Friendship Matters

On behalf of

Thank you for attending
Laughing Your Way to Better Health...Seriously!
March 6, 2018

Friendship Matters

memoir, life lessons, laughter

SANDA NESHIN BERNSTEIN, PSY.D.
WENDY SATIN RAPAPORT, PSY.D., L.C.S.W.

PSYCHOLOGISTS and FRIENDS

ISBN: 1537317350
ISBN 13: 9781537317359
Library of Congress Control Number: 2016917516
CreateSpace Independent Publishing Platform
North Charleston, South Carolina
Front cover designed by Ariel Rutland

Some people go to priests, others to poetry, I to my friends -

VIRGINIA WOOLF

There is nothing better than a friend, unless it is a friend with chocolate-

LINDA GRAYSON

Friendship Matters

Contents

Introduction

Don't walk behind me; I may not lead. Don't walk in front of me; I may not follow. Just walk beside me and be my friend.

-ALBERT CAMUS

FRIENDSHIP MATTERS.

Everyone knows that.

Sometimes we underestimate the potential of what friends do for us and how we mutually benefit by being that special friend in return.

In this book, we want to remind you of friendship's documented *superpowers*: improved health and longevity;

enhanced competence in relationships and decision making; and the pleasure of a sweet loving connection.

Many of us have friends who touch different parts of our lives. We have friends we go running with, friends from our book club, friends at work, and friends who fit well when we are part of a couple. All of these friends are important to us; all *matter.* But sometimes, if we're lucky to have found a person with whom we click, and we are motivated to invest in that relationship, we can create a different kind of friendship. We can have that rare friend who is connected to us from deep inside each of us. She knows our vulnerabilities as well as our strengths. And we know hers. There is no shame, no embarrassment, just acceptance. And admiration. (Not to mention a loving nudge when she notices we are off our chosen path.)

We are writing this book because we "found" each other and cultivated that rare kind of friendship. And we want to describe it to you. We have been amazed by the power of our friendship to have such a positive impact on all of our relationships.

When we met long ago, we never anticipated that our friendship would go this deep and last so long. After all these decades, we began to ask ourselves: What has made it work so well? What exactly does friendship do for us? Can we share what we've learned in a way that may be useful to others seeking meaningful and intimate relationships with friends?

We should disclose at this point that we are both trained as psychologists, so curiosity about the "how" of our friendship fits very well into how we think. Because we are practicing psychologists and have been in god - knows how many years of therapy between us, our friendship involves a particular way of understanding and supporting each other. Our conversations reflect this. But believe us, you don't need to be a psychologist or a therapist to develop this kind of friendship. And the friendship doesn't have to be lifelong, like ours. You can use these ideas and skills with someone you meet early in your life as well as with friends you meet later in life. You can use these skills starting now.

Everyone can learn. Perhaps you already feel successful in these ways but still want to deepen your friendship, to become more empathic, more appreciative of your differences, and more honest about your feelings. We think that we have a lot to offer you. And our ideas and skills are universally accessible and possible to master, even if you have had difficulty in the past trusting and sharing with another.

But you'll see. We want you to listen in to our *process - how* we speak to each other. We think that our friendship, a *conscious friendship,* has made each of us emotionally stronger, more effective in our relationships with others, and more self-reliant.

It's valuable to have someone in life in addition to a spouse, partner, child, or parent with whom there is committed caring. That friend can remind you to hold on to *you* - keeping the healthy selfishness alive - as she also reinforces empathic understanding of others.

This book is very personal. It begins with a story involving the two of us. By telling it, we hope you can see the give -and-take that goes on between us as we try to help one another. We hope too that this will make the book all the more vivid and therefore more accessible to you. We want our book to serve as a catalyst for you to expand your own friendships.

We then go on to tell you a little about who we are and invite you to listen in to our conversation. In that way you can begin to have a greater sense of our friendship. Throughout, we will underscore the importance of *having a special friend*. With that person you will learn how to understand **emotional literacy** (the ability to know and regulate your emotions as well as empathize with others' experiences.) Together you will transform the concept of the **good mother** (a person who loves you, wants the best for you, and always has your back) into a real-life ongoing part of your relationships. As you are acquiring the satisfaction that emotional literacy and good mothering add to your friendship, we will also help you choose a stance of ***open-mindedness*** and ***open-heartedness*** in the world rather than an inhibited, self-protective, or critical view.

Next we will ask you to wrap your mind around a group of ideas, which are the "how" or "strategies" of our friendship, all flowing from the concept of openness. You probably have thought of these concepts at various moments, but we put them together in a sequence that is easier to remember by its ABC structure. (As you can imagine, we were perfectly behaved in elementary school.) We hope you will keep them strung together to assure an easier way of being in yourself and in the world. Here they are, in alphabetical order:

A. Assumptions: Don't make them without checking it out
B. Boundaries: Make them strong and flexible
C. Criticism: Learn to give and to receive it
D. Differences: Appreciate them. No, really
E. Empathy: Widen your lens and understand the other
F. Forgiveness: Let go and move on
G. Gratitude: Go for joy

We consciously use these guidelines and want to share them with you... and your friends. We will share situations from our everyday lives to illustrate our ideas. You will notice that our examples are not dramatic; they are simple but nuanced. That's our point.

Our friendship has been a pleasure, a lifesaver, and in retrospect a *laboratory* for figuring out ways to improve relationships with the world around us and with ourselves.

Please read on and see how you might deepen your friendships to enhance your lives too. You may not have someone in mind, or you may wonder who is capable or even willing and interested to do the work of friendship with you. Perhaps give a copy of this book to someone who might become that special friend and see what happens.

Now a word about how we want you to read this book. Pause and take a deep breath after reading each chapter. We hope to engage your emotions as well as stimulate your mind. We want you to look at possibly familiar concepts in a new way. (Don't worry, it's a small book.) Seriously, please don't rush; we want you to absorb our points slowly. Perhaps read the chapters in brief spurts so that you are not either bored or overwhelmed. Resist any urge you feel to write off the parts that may at first feel too difficult or too idealistic. (We have been accused of being seasoned practitioners of positivity; one of us happily accepts this diagnosis as a badge of honor.)

Remember too that for all of us human beings, learning new ideas and behaviors is never easy. Think "baby steps." Change begets change incrementally. Just as our bodies develop muscle memory for a sport after many hours of focused practice, altering the way we look at things, speak to ourselves, and interact with the world similarly requires *intention, mindfulness, and practice.*

Remember that the two of us have been working at this for a very long time, politely policing each other along the way.

Our friendship *matters.*

We are excited to share the *matters* of our friendship.

1

EVERYONE NEEDS A FRIEND
(but not everyone needs a ukulele)

SANDY: WE BEGIN with a story of how an innocent and funny exchange, a small issue really, came to highlight for us the complexity of understanding what goes on *within* and *between* people, especially when there is the possibility for conflict.

WENDY: Okay. The ukulele story. It happened very recently and goes like this:

I have a bright and shiny orange ukulele. I love it. When I see it on the stand, I smile because I bought it under my daughter-in-law Teri's influence. I pick it up and primitively strum and sing old folk songs (not *old folk* songs- though they are starting to mean the same thing) with my "good enough" voice. It brings me so much joy. You are visiting,

Sandy, and I want you to play the ukulele, too. I want you to have a touch of the same thrill I have. I offer it to you several times over the weekend and teach you a chord. (It only takes 3 chords to play 200 songs.) I haven't told you but I am already planning to send you a new ukulele of your very own, and if we weren't writing this book, it would have been in the mail at the same moment you smiled as you sang *500 Miles* with me.

Readers, are you with me? Can you feel my simple purity of thought and desire -at least as I felt it- my spontaneous generosity? But wait, slow down. My gesture is rejected. Sandy says she doesn't want me to give her a ukulele.

She's gotta be kidding.

Oops, maybe not.

How could my giving a gift to my dearest friend ever be a problem? I am crushed, stopped in my impulsive tracks. I am shocked at how the simplicity of my gift, given in the most straightforward sense of: *Share my joy...perhaps like it as much as I do...enjoy seeing it as an object d'arte or a memory of a care free time and definitely-feel the love.* Seriously, how could that evoke any hint of annoyance in you, the receiver? Those are my **intentions.** But I am beginning to understand, however, that Sandy's **perceptions** just might be different. I don't want to but it is Sandy so I force myself to stay open to her reaction.

SANDY: I explain that this simple gift for me, initially at least, brings with it uncomfortable feelings: I am being told what to do (Hello, childhood experiences!); the implications are that I must learn something that's not of my choosing; and I must send a gift in return. I felt your gift put pressure on me.

WENDY: So now, as in all uncomfortable interactions, we have to share our "process"-what goes on *inside* ourselves and *between* us. I swear it's not boring -though it is work- very necessary and pleasantly tedious work. Take note that this is our *slow-motion* exercise in communication which we highly recommend.

Here we go. We try to identify, understand, and express our individual feelings and intentions in giving and receiving, all in the name of loving and growing. We choose this consciously because without being mindful of our intentions as well as considering how our desires affect each other, we may end up becoming angry, feeling rejected or misunderstood.

The conversation:

WENDY: *I have to tell you how much I want to send it to you.*

SANDY: *I have to tell you how much I want you to wait.*

WENDY: I really am listening to you. I feel the strain of considering that I am being asked to change my usual response. Damn, giving a gift requires work and incredible sensitivity. I know now that the free spirit of my sending doesn't always penetrate the other with joy. When should I ask permission to send my gift? And, on the other hand, when should I insist that you learn something important to me that I believe will stretch you in a good way? Can I ever insist?

In our differences the questions cause us to weigh pleasing ourselves or pleasing the other. And is there a way we can do both?

SANDY: Can you pause ...to see if I am willing to expand myself according to your desire? And if my continued inclination is no, can you accept my right to refuse and see it as a statement about me and not a rejection of you? And can you still feel that we each love and accept the other always, even if I don't want your offering at this moment?

WENDY: Well, yes, but at least your response should remind you of my intent, that you "see" me at the same time as you take care of yourself. It might begin with *I love that you thought of me.*

Newsflash...Breaking news. I am getting a burst of pleasure from the conscious self-control I am exercising in not sending the gift. I pause and think it through with some of Sandy's nuance and I feel a certain satisfaction in my discipline.

SANDY: Yes, I can imagine that. At the same time I can now also imagine that owning the ukulele doesn't have to feel like something imposed on me. I can use it or not, however I want, knowing it has made you happy just to share one of your pleasures with me. Even as I'm writing this, Wendy, I still have that old feeling of being told what to do and my old resistance to it. It's such hard work to see it from another vantage point, yours. That is, I understand where you're coming from, but it's hard for me to shake up my own deeply held, though probably no-longer -helpful feelings.

WENDY: I love that you are making us realize how hard it is to change, for both of us. I felt ashamed for a moment about my impulsiveness, an old feeling, but sharing your self-awareness with me makes me realize I don't have to hold on to that embarrassment. Perhaps I first need to better appreciate the personal history behind my need to make people happy, and as I do so, to think about in what ways that has kept me from paying enough attention to my own needs. This conversation with you is teaching me to expand my repertoire.

Sandy, you don't think it means I have to send recall notices to people from my past to whom I have sent ukuleles...

SANDY: Could you? No, no. It's ironic that discussing our differences only makes me feel closer to you. I might be annoyed at your persistence, but I feel known by you and known more clearly to myself.

But don't send the ukulele yet!

WENDY: While this story highlights many of the atti- tudes toward life we will be describing in this book, the main highlight is the **power of the relationship** - the power of friendship to encourage us to know ourselves, to make ourselves hardy- not to mention happy, and still be open to change. We didn't stay uncomfortable with one another be- cause we really feel an underlying love and acceptance. We have a pledge to never stay insulted or defensive with one another, even if that is sometimes our first response. We want you to notice how our friendship cocoons us with love and acceptance and how that enables us to challenge one another and ourselves. We know how hard it is to be open to change without first feeling loved and accepted.

2

OUR FRIENDSHIP --Once
upon a time...

SANDY: PEOPLE OFTEN ask us how we met and whether we knew immediately that ours would become a special friendship. I remember specifically when and how we met but I don't think I had any way back then to imagine how deeply we would be woven into the fabric of each other's lives and how our conversations would continue over a lifetime.

WENDY: You know how people tell the story of how they first met -delicious for them but how boring and tedious it can be for others? Our sincerest apologies, if necessary. We can't help ourselves (because we don't want to). So, here we go.

The year was 1969. It was a transformative decade and a particularly intense year.

SANDY: Woodstock, the moon landing, anti-war protests, women's liberation, women's consciousness raising groups, communes. OMG, I remember those times so well. I had transferred in 1967 from my small women's college in Massachusetts, where I was having demitasse every evening and following that with a game of badly-played bridge, to Barnard College in New York City, part of Columbia University. I arrived just in time to watch the strikes - I can still hear the chanting as the students manned the barricades and unbelievably took over the University. Classes were cancelled. The president of the University resigned.

What a cultural chasm I had to leap across.

WENDY: I know. They were unnerving though very exciting times. My freshman year at George Washington University, I was enjoying museums and prosaic politics working for Representative Claude Pepper. When I transferred to the University of Miami, we were picketing the administration building and seeking equal rights for black students. Hey, Sandy, you can say you went to Smith for college. I get esteem from saying I have a friend who went to Smith College.

SANDY: Seriously? Anyway, it was a cold autumn afternoon in New York City. I was pregnant with my first child.

You, Wendy, and your then- husband Charlie had recently arrived from Florida, where you both had grown up. You didn't have a proper winter coat. For some reason that stuck with me.

WENDY: Perhaps that was your instinctive mothering, wanting to keep me warm, particularly as I had grown up with Miami Beach blood.

SANDY: Hmm...maybe. But it was cold and you had some flimsy jacket, definitely not up to New York weather. We were with our husbands going to hear a lecture at NYU Law School, where Charlie was a student. We both had to go to the restroom so we started off together, chatting amiably along the way. My clear memory is of the sound of us peeing in adjoining stalls intermixed with our ongoing conversation. No embarrassment, no polite silence; we just never stopped talking. And here we are, still talking almost 50 years later.

WENDY: Here's my version. We fell in love at first sight. Sandy, you were pregnant. Within five minutes of meeting, not unexpectedly, you had to go to the bathroom, so we went together. We continued talking, well into the stalls -when most people appropriately would have stopped talking to guarantee a presumed desire for privacy.

SANDY: It was the two couples who first became close. We even had planned that in the future we would live together commune-style. You and I were busy with our individual lives - I was with a newborn, you were teaching. And then after a few years you and Charlie returned to Florida to live. We didn't see one another. Yet we stayed friends. It makes me wonder, why we did remain important to one another, and increasingly so.

WENDY: It was unique right from the beginning...we were both so alike, so curious about ideas in similar ways, yet so different in temperament and physical appearance -- me a tall, dark-haired, extrovert and you a shy, quieter blonde. If I ever have to pick an actress to play me in a movie, it might be Beyonce or Jennifer Lopez. Who else for a nice voluptuous and expressive Jewish girl? (Okay, so maybe Lainie Kazan, who stars as a Greek woman who has probably been on a diet her whole life, as I have.) And for you...

SANDY: Do we have to typecast me? Please, no.

WENDY: I heard you say no before you said it. You have never understood yourself to be as deeply thoughtful, beautiful, and perpetually in great shape as you are.

.

SANDY: NO! NO! NO! You must be kidding. That description is not me. Let's move on to the important stuff that brought us together.

WENDY: We were in your tiny kitchen and somehow you were able to ask me big and intimate questions about how I felt about things and how I had come to those points of view: love, friendship, the war, the draft, women's rights. You made me dig deep in myself to how I felt and thought. (You were an analyst before you were an analyst.)

SANDY: I don't think I asked anyone else those questions, so why you? I think there was something about your willingness to be open.

WENDY: And happily self-deprecating.

SANDY: No, open and willing to share *vulnerability* right from the start. And I loved that about you. For me, it was such an invitation to enter, to enter an intimacy in which I could explore my own self as well. That was compelling.

WENDY: You are right. Our lives changed and differences could have kept us apart- geography, marital status, children status - but they didn't. We were engaged in a conversation about our *inner thoughts,* a safe partnership of self-exploration. I actually never knew details about what your house looked like, (though I assumed you made your own curtains out of gingham), where you shopped and whether you looked for sales, what books or movies were part of your life; or -- here's a dangerous thought -- whether you had any other friends.

SANDY: That's true, isn't it? We didn't share too much about the details of our lives back then. But just for the record, they were not gingham curtains. They were made of gold-colored burlap, if we're being precise. I remember buying yards of that inexpensive fabric and lugging it, coarse, itchy, heavy as it was, on the interminable subway ride back to my Queens apartment and to my sewing machine. And as for me knowing your life, I knew that you liked to buy lots of costume jewelry which you wore when I did see you in such fabulous out-there ways; and that you and Charlie were social activists, involved in civil rights causes and anti-war demonstrations. As far as other friends, I think we didn't share much back then. Maybe we weren't yet able to tolerate and talk about our ambivalent feelings: jealousy as well as happiness for one another.

WENDY: In our phone calls, we both had a desire to end every conversation just a little bit smarter or stronger than the beginning of the phone call. (Note my tendency to romantic exaggeration.)

SANDY: Ha! I don't think so--about the smarter, stronger part. Maybe you did. But I do think we saw that our friendship could be a source of helping us grow as human beings. And we both were invested in growing. And besides, we laughed a lot!

WENDY: My memory of why we became so close was through feeling you *liked* me- even though you knew my insecurities. I never felt judged - and at the same time, you could give me criticisms when you felt I didn't come through for you (*"How could you be in New York and not call me?"*). You asked me to be self-reflective rather than just being disappointed in me. You wanted to understand me and you wanted me to be more committed, to explain myself when I couldn't stand up and come through for myself or you or us. I liked what you asked of me.

SANDY: I think that I admired the ways in which you were very different from me. You seemed braver than I felt able to be with people; you seemed to say what was on your mind more easily than I did. I was intrigued by that. You were curious about how I understood people's emotions, especially our own. I felt that you admired me and liked me and didn't mind sharing even embarrassing experiences. For example, remember the time that you....

WENDY: Don't even think about it... I am not going to share specifics with all our readers. I love that by speaking on the phone regularly we found a way to remain constant in each other's lives even though we have always lived in different places, me in Florida and Maine and you in New York. In the early years, we had to talk quickly since long distance phone calls were exorbitantly expensive. Years later, we began to supplement our phone conversations with deliberate weekends together twice a year. While I mostly remember those weekends as one long conversation, trying to satisfy our seemingly unquenchable thirst for connection, I also remember how we experimented with a variety of experiences and adventures on those weekends.

SANDY: In my mind's eye I can see us perched high on rocks overlooking Camden Harbor in midcoast Maine, each of us with paintbrush in hand. You had bought us watercolor kits from Wal-Mart and we were trying to find the combination of blues that best matched our cloudless sky.

WENDY: Seriously, who knew that blue came in so many colors.

SANDY: And don't forget when we rented kayaks in Kennebunkport with the swirling ocean current suddenly and frighteningly stronger than we were, pulling us out to sea while we were furiously paddling as we tried to save ourselves.

WENDY: Yes, that's the time we did last rites and decided to stick to talking and laughing and an occasional massage, limiting the danger. (That's where my fear base overpowered the friendship.)

SANDY: No, no. You are being modest and going for a cheap shot with your humor. We have been hiking, biking, and sailing. We have gone to poetry class and taken a weekend writing course when we first thought about writing together. (It was "Writing From The Inside Out," a good match for two psychologists.) We have managed to cram a lot of living into our brief "same time next year" weekends together.

WENDY: Meanwhile, these days, we speak about whatever strikes us, once a week. We still muse over the literary or political issues of the day, laugh joyfully over who remembers what, share the details of our family and professional lives, and, of course, recite the well-known pangs of insecurity engendered by some unexpected insult in our daily lives. Remember when I couldn't wait to talk to you because a colleague I had trained years ago recently criticized my professional slides?

SANDY: And I felt so relieved to be able to talk to you after my apartment house neighbor of 6 years failed to recognize me when I returned home the other day. The potential insults are always there.

WENDY: Sometimes it's just our take on it.

SANDY: And sometimes it's intentional. You remember "mean" girls. But seriously, I know it's usually not intentional.

WENDY: These conversations make me smile. We enjoy our history, deep understanding, and much requited love and admiration. I know you will insist me back into security with your listening and your words. I know you will be there so I postpone my angst until our call, assured that you will "get me" and turn me around or listen intently until I pick myself up.

One might think I'd be over insecurity at this point.

SANDY: Ahem. You know it's not possible to end insecurity permanently. We can all be vulnerable at times, particularly to the same old issues. I can still feel insecure when a friend doesn't make plans with me when I expected her to.

WENDY: The need for approval and love never leaves us; mostly that's a good thing. I try to recognize my triggers and I do seem to bounce back more quickly now to either act differently in the first place or to make amends, especially with your support.

SANDY: I appreciate that you feel that way about the meaning of our friendship. And I know so well what you mean. You encourage me to speak up, to act, when I might want to avoid. You say that I help you to slow down, to look at situations in a more nuanced way, before you act on them. Perhaps I do. In turn, you help me to see the power of not taking the first no for an answer, to see the power of persistence.

So, Wendy, we have in one another a friend who knows us, who admires us, who loves us, and who complements us.

WENDY: Not to mention someone who buoys us up in the face of outside stress and who challenges us with new ways of thinking about situations.

SANDY: We help one another turn toward happiness and optimism.

At the same time, being friends does not mean that we always agree with one another. Or even that we see things similarly. Over the years we have come to appreciate and learn from our core differences in temperament and point of view.

WENDY: I like to confront issues head- on, probably way too immediately, and you like to step back and reflect before engaging. Sometimes I wince before I hear your thoughts when I know we might disagree in politics or I know I have handled something in a way that I could have done better. I know we are going to challenge each other's thinking.

SANDY: You wince, really? I so appreciate the opportunity we give one another to expand our thinking without making each other feel stupid or wrong.

WENDY: I have broad shoulders which hide an occasionally timid soul. But yes, of course, I feel safe, after my initial reaction.

SANDY: We truly are interested in growing from each other. Not into each other.

WENDY: You know, we all look in the mirror. Sometimes we grimace or find fault, but we're in trouble if we don't walk away with a sense of looking "good enough" or having a reasonable plan to change what we don't like. Thanks, Sandy, for helping me in that way.

So, readers, in this book Sandy and I want to partner with you as we do with each other. We want to be the parents who tuck your hand safely and warmly in theirs, so you can look more deeply in the mirror and see yourself with compassion and with the possibility for change. Our hope for you is that you have a friend who partners with you in the way we so value.

Takeaway

- Everyone needs and benefits from having a friend.
- Take time to listen in *slow motion* to one another; it takes time, commitment, and effort to understand each other.
- Learn to respect and enjoy your *differences.*

3

WITH A FRIEND -- Take this short course on EMOTIONAL LITERACY

WENDY: LET ME begin by sharing an interaction that involves my loving husband Jim. Please note that despite the following example, we have had 26 intimate and extremely happy years so far.

Sometimes when I am with him and something breaks - be it something as simple as a wine glass or as complex as a dishwasher, either accidentally or because things break- he may say, "What did **you** do that made that break?" When I'm feeling insecure, Jim's comment may leave me feeling scolded, ashamed, and small. Did I do something wrong? Was I a bad girl? And being Wendy, with my own unique emotional response patterns, I may then feel a short temper tantrum coming on (not involving throwing things other than words) and want to yell at Jim for the bad feeling that his comment engenders in me. This is when I need to work hard to manage not having an outburst because it's not fair to him or good for me.

SANDY: Yes, time to pause here and figure out what's going on inside, with your own emotions. This is the beginning step of *emotional literacy*.

WENDY: Can I be a teacher for a moment....bear with me...and excuse me for the didactic or overbearing quality but I want us to be really clear about emotional literacy.

Don't you love how I apologize *before* I annoy?

Emotional literacy begins with developing our ability to *recognize* and understand our own emotions. (*Self-awareness*) We learn to *listen* carefully to what we say to ourselves (*Self-talk*) so we can begin to manage our negative and self-defeating thoughts and feelings. (*Self-Regulation*) This requires having feeling for, i.e. interest and concern, (*Compassion*) for our own response and for others. Next we try to take a moment to feel and understand how the experience might be for the other person. (*Empathy*). With that empathy, we try to more effectively communicate both positive and difficult feelings. (*Express*)

SANDY: That's a lot to do before we allow ourselves to speak.

WENDY: It only takes a moment...but not at first. It takes practice.

SANDY: Let's go back to your example so this process comes to life.

WENDY: When I am in a good and steady place, feeling loved and self- confident, it's easier for me to deal with emotional and interpersonal challenges, like feeling hurt by Jim's comment. When I am comfortable with myself I can acknowledge my feelings, and laugh to myself. (It makes me so aware how we tend to repeat what we heard as children.) In fact, I might not discuss it at all.

But if I am not feeling so secure, I need to stop longer to *identify* the feelings and check out my emotional response. I try to recognize what I might be feeling - somewhere on the spectrum of shame, hurt or anger(*self-awareness.*) After I check out my feelings, with compassion, I take a moment to imagine what childhood or current experiences may have triggered Jim's response. Rather than reacting with attack or withdrawal, I consciously decide to look at it differently for myself and for Jim (*empathy* for both of us) and then on to *self-regulation.*

In the case of not feeling so solid, I try to take a moment to remember how mutually respectful we usually are to each other and recognize that this is a different reaction from Jim. I realize his initial comment may be triggered by his own issues, not mine. (Watch out: This is not always true; sometimes it *is* about you!) I can breathe a sigh of relief and know I don't have to take it personally.

Then I can warmly and playfully say - to bring me to comfort, "Why, Jim, sweetheart, things break. You poor baby. Did someone shame you when you were a kid? Whoever did that to you when you were growing up might have been feeling so close to the last straw, and of course, while they might have been remorseful (or not), how difficult for you. You were a good kid and things break. And that also means, I am still a good kid when things break."

SANDY: You're kidding, right! I may love your outcome, I don't know. But I would never say that whole "therapeutically-skilled" but to me stilted and- excuse my language- preachy sentence.

WENDY: I deserve that. Maybe. I didn't realize until you called me on it. I see now my words conveyed very thinly veiled hostility which came out as condescension. This tends to happen when I don't give myself enough time to allow for and then manage my initial resentment.

SANDY: Good point. As always, there are so many emotions operating at the same time. It takes a while to sort them out. But I'm also struck by our different strategies to get to the same goal of empathy for the other while never losing empathy for ourselves. I could never speak like you did to Jim, even playfully. I wouldn't want to; it's not my style. But I would still be talking to myself if I were in your place, saying to myself that this is Jim's issue--not mine. I guess it's important to recognize that there are real individual differences in how each of us will manage our emotions.

WENDY: Yes, I can see that sometimes my responses sound a bit contrived, though for me it is part of *regulating* my response by perhaps stiltedly talking it out. I am trying to find compassion for Jim as well as myself. The benefit for both of us is that I can stop myself from being angry. I say the words and by the time I finish - I actually mean them.

SANDY: Interesting. Often, although not always, I too can do that for myself by thinking those thoughts without saying them. You were kind to Jim as well in that you didn't react angrily. Of course, after all that forced listening, he is probably saying, "What the $#@% is she talking about?"

WENDY: Yes. I empathized with how that felt to Jim, but I missed giving him a chance to both understand my feelings (once I recognized them and even told him) and truly also remember and have compassion for his from the past - *reexamine his old response pattern,* whether he thought he needed it or not. Poor guy. Imagine being married to a psychologist who insists on being a teacher.

SANDY: Your point is such a good one. I too, when I talk only to myself, miss the chance to allow the other person to understand my feelings as well as her own. I should try to remember the downside to handling issues like this by myself only.

WENDY: Yes, with these conversations we are preventing and--if need be--repairing the potential damage that disappointment, hurt, or conflict can do to a relationship.

SANDY: Okay, so we become aware of our emotions and manage them by slowing ourselves down, by trying not to react first. You may do that by talking it out with the person. I may talk to myself. (I often do.)

For example, I've already mentioned that I may feel slighted when a friend doesn't return my call. Rather than being left with annoyance, which may tempt me to answer less than happily when she does call, I try to develop a more enlightened and effective path, one that might keep me from feeling the initial hurt that lies beneath the annoyance.

WENDY: What do you do at that point? (I think I might need some coaching on this, too.)

SANDY: I might say to myself, "*I'm going to try to understand why she might not have called back without taking it personally.*" I try to make myself generate alternative explanations to "widen my lens" in understanding her behavior. Maybe she is very busy. Maybe she is preoccupied with important issues in her own life. Maybe she is depressed and has isolated herself.

WENDY: Yes, that works. But talking *with* someone- be it the person in the situation at the time or to a friend - is an extra guarantee, in difficult situations, that you aren't reinforcing negative or unhelpful thoughts. It's important that we identify our own *hotspots* or *triggers*, and be empathic.

SANDY: And by empathy we mean taking a moment to have compassionate observation and acceptance -without judgment. It's not "giving up" your position; it's enlarging your perspective. It's not easy to do but it's important, so important that we're going to devote a separate chapter to empathy later in this book. As we're discussing this, I'm reminded of a time when I was pretty weak in having those skills. I had hurt feelings and managed them with avoidance instead of doing something more mature and productive. It's a long-ago example but one that I've repeated many times since. It feels embarrassing to tell...

WENDY: Embarrassed? Where's your compassion for yourself?

SANDY: Okay. Okay. So here I was, a young married woman with two small children working part-time only. I was asked to write an article on the topic of "Can Women Have It All?" by a dynamic and creative friend who lived down the block in my suburban Long Island neighborhood. Jane was a woman I greatly admired who had started her own feminist newspaper. I was flattered to be asked to write. I was excited about identifying with feminist causes. So imagine how disappointed I was when the article was rejected. I was told it needed considerable editing before it could be resubmitted.

WENDY: Ouch for you! Remember Sandy, it wasn't actually rejected, just not ready for print yet. You were used to being smart and getting things right with minimal effort. What a shock to learn how much effort has to go into most challenges to be successful. (Duh.)

SANDY: So, instead of being able to say to myself, "*Okay, it hurts that my first draft wasn't acceptable, but I need to try again because if I continue my efforts, I stand a good chance of being successful,*" instead of saying that, I simply said to myself that I was too busy to rewrite. I avoided confronting my pain as I simultaneously made any experience of success impossible.

WENDY: I wish I had known about it way back then. I wouldn't have let you give up. Excuse my grandiosity in thinking I could change you, but I would have wanted us to have an important conversation. I might have reminded you that you could allow yourself to feel the pain, see it differently, and then really *choose* a path instead of just letting it happen to you. We could have a good laugh about how the jig was up, how you had to do rewrites for the first time in your life, and that meant you were still the brain, but it required work.

We both know defenses such as blaming the other guy or avoiding can cost a lot. Not only might you miss the "good stuff," as in having a successfully published article, but you might not see the opportunity in criticism. Maybe there's something in any feedback that you really should be willing to at least look at. But you must still retain a solid sense of yourself while you look.

SANDY: Of course, from this perspective I can see that you're right. And I know that handling my hurt feelings with compassion and rational thought would have helped. But at least as important was that I should have reached out to you, my friend, to help me do what I was having difficulty doing for myself.

WENDY: Yes! And I would have also reminded you that emotions tend to pass. Your hurt feelings will pass. Like it or not, it's the way of emotions: Good emotions pass, unfortunately, and luckily so do negative emotions.

SANDY: There's one more point I want to make here. Handling and expressing emotions well isn't *just* a set of skills that everyone learns to apply with equal ease or effectiveness. Like it or not, we are shaped by our past histories and by our biology. This may affect how intensely we feel our emotions and how effectively we can regulate and manage them. We don't all begin at the same starting point, and early life experiences, as well as culture, significantly impact us in very individual ways.

For example, I was by inborn temperament a shy, easily frightened, overly sensitive child. I was highly reactive to all stimuli - loud noises, strong lights, as well as change. Growing up, my experience of my mother's voice as she disciplined us was that it was loud and scary.

WENDY: How about some perspective for yourself here? Maybe you were sensitive, not overly sensitive. This is a sidebar, but the upside of this for you has been advantageous in you being the empathic professional and person that you are, don't you think?

SANDY: Yeah. Yeah. Yeah. But stay with me for a moment and realize how difficult it felt for me growing up.

WENDY: So you need me to soothe you first, not immediately "inform" you of another way to look at it. *Soothe not inform.* Got it. Seriously, this is emotional literacy at its best.

SANDY: I was anxious and frightened a lot. Even today it can be difficult for me to handle criticism expressed in what I perceive to be a loud voice. Isn't that amazing, I sometimes say to myself, all these years later, with all my self-awareness at the ready, and I am still emotionally vulnerable to dynamics that were imprinted on me when I was a young child. That's what I want our readers to understand. *That our pasts are always with us* to some extent. Because of this, our reactions don't always match what is needed in the current situation. They may be over or under reactive - or miss the mark entirely.

We can and must be kind to ourselves (in all the ways this book suggests) but we must also come to accept that we have been shaped by our pasts in ways that can be modified and regulated but probably will never totally disappear. So, most of us at one time or another can go to a place where we feel less than valuable and less than lovable, as I can do when I'm criticized. That feeling of being vulnerable, some of us can go there more quickly than others and stay there longer, but all of us, at one time or another, will experience it, along with a variety of other unpleasant feelings - shame, embarrassment, hurt, anger, fear.

WENDY: *These are a few of my favorite things...* Don't go too dark here, Sandy. Being vulnerable can also make us able to be empathic, to expand ourselves by understanding where another person is coming from, to be closer, to love more deeply. Being vulnerable can unfortunately also lead people to stay away from deep connection.

SANDY: Yes, I agree. That way they don't feel vulnerable to loss. It's human nature to want to avoid feeling pain. We tend to try to protect ourselves from feeling vulnerable in more or less healthy ways. For example, if I can lessen the sting of criticism leveled at me by being angry at the person expressing it, I might not feel as bad about myself: "*Who do you think you are, talking to me like that!!*"

WENDY: Yes, and we know that there are healthy, more adaptive responses to protect our vulnerable emotions and keep us from feeling devastated or deepening the conflict. Blaming the other is not a healthy choice, however good it might feel in the short term. I always try to remind myself that when I can listen with empathy, I can gain perspective and allow myself to understand and hear the other person's discomfort rather than taking the words personally.

Don't you think perhaps we need to be less afraid of our vulnerability and our difficult feelings? There is a place for them; they provide information to understand more about ourselves or the other person.

SANDY: You're saying something so important here, Wendy. Sometimes I have to say to myself, I won't "die" from my hurt and vulnerable feelings. Maybe if I can tolerate the hurt, I can learn something useful. At the same time, and even though at some level I know all that, the truth is that sometimes I just don't want to hear it.

WENDY: Good reminder. That's how others may feel about our comments too. Note to self: Allow for some sulking time. I forget that almost all of us need a moment before we feel like being empathic. (Pollyanna has been ordered to her room for a temporary halt.)

Takeaway

- Know how your own emotions function. Learn how to "read" and regulate yourself. Take time to know your *self-talk* and tune in to see how others feel too.
- Cultivate compassion and empathy - for yourself as well as the other person- when you are dealing with difficult interactions and uncomfortable feelings (anger, resentment, guilt, etc.)
- Recognize your *hotspots* and *triggers;* be aware they may be related to childhood experiences and genetics and may take more effort to master.

4

EMOTIONAL LITERACY Part 2: Not a short course when you add envy

SANDY: As LONG as Pollyanna isn't here, dare I mention the "darker" emotions of envy and jealousy as well as competitiveness? Those feelings occur normally in relationships. You and I don't spend much time there, I don't think, and yet perhaps we need to ask ourselves why.

WENDY: Maybe living far apart, being so physically different (equal but separate beauty), never drinking too much when we are together, and having very good communication *habits* ... all contribute to minimizing our natural competition.

SANDY: I know I have felt and can still feel envy of your quick-wittedness, your ability to make people laugh as well as your incredible ability to speak to every person in an auditorium of 500 and make each person feel connected to you, laughing all the way. And how about when you recently were recognized in your high school as an outstanding graduate, inducted, as very, very few are, into the Miami Beach High School Hall of Fame. I flew down to celebrate the event with you. Yet, somehow, even though I can feel initial envy, I come to feel it more as admiration for your amazing achievements.

Maybe it's a matter of maturity and mutual acceptance. We have come to know who we are and to accept ourselves in part because we are accepted and valued by one another and in part because we are a lot more confident in the world than we were when we were younger. The difficult feelings are there but they don't seem to get in the way. They are part of many other more loving feelings. Is that still Pollyanna here in the room with us?

WENDY: I like what you are saying--not just the nice things about me, but the sense of mutual admiration that lessens the power of my envy of you. Your intelligence intimidated me in the beginning. Now, for example, I feel envy and then relief at your ability to be steady and thoughtful; you always want to know more to avoid being prematurely reactive.

I think of envy and competition as *controlled substances* -needing extreme caution and oversight in allowing them into my own life as well as between us, Sandy.

SANDY: Hold on. Extreme caution seems a bit too.... extreme? Competition can serve us well; it can be a positive motivator. I think that sometimes I convert my envy and competitiveness towards you into motivation to be more like you in certain ways, in your interpersonal style of being out there and engaged.

WENDY: I know, me too. (That sounds competitive. It's not a dirty word). I often imagine my envy of your analytic and intellectual strengths putting a muzzle on my "let's act" muscle. I ration it and use it-as needed-as part of a "stimulus package" when I think I can benefit from some change.

SANDY: And as for real competition, if I were at all athletic, I truly believe I would be happy to beat you in a game of tennis. (Okay, I know that's a total fantasy for me... it's not going to happen.)

WENDY: I am pretty sure I would have to throw the game to you. (Who am I kidding...as if I could actually win?) My older sister Mary Ellen teases me that Serena Williams - in one of her first competitions as a tennis star pitted against her older sister - may have *let* Venus win. I get it; sometimes I would rather be liked than first.

I can give faint recognition to difficult feelings - like envy, jealousy, or competition. Often they have only a dim light on them; I brush them off in a rapid and underground manner. In my positivity vein, sometimes I experience just plain vicarious pleasure in another's joys.

SANDY: There will always be aspects of another person, be it appearance, money, weight, exercise, or success that are possible target areas for envy and competition.

WENDY: Yes. You and I have experienced difficult feelings toward one another in all these areas over the course of our friendship and we have learned to handle those feelings well, helping each other to grow as we did so. Self-awareness is key. I try to pay attention and recognize my own envy or competitiveness as *information*, as normal and even possibly valuable. I learn to let go of the feelings that are not helpful or interfere in the friendship. For example, I no longer fantasize about going to Smith College.

SANDY: You're teasing here but how big are your underlying feelings of jealousy or envy and what should I do when I hear them? Your words make me wonder. Should we ever discuss our feelings of envy with a friend? I don't want to give up the pleasure in my successful feelings in order to protect you from envy.

WENDY: Of course not! I would want you sturdy and satisfied if I needed to talk to you. No guilt, anger or shame- that *stays*, anyhow- in either direction.

SANDY: And I would want you sturdy enough to handle your own negative emotions. So should I bring up the issue at all? Maybe not. Maybe teasing is a good way of managing the more difficult feelings that are only one part of a greater, more nuanced set of feelings. I for my part certainly know how it feels to experience envy of you... So maybe when I recognize that, and recognize that you are successfully handling your envy, I can just laugh with you. It's only if either one of us feels that the issues are interfering that we need to address them.

WENDY: If we need to talk, we stay present for how this conversation can make both of us feel. For difficult feelings to be shared, humor and "play" are good ways to get a challenging conversation started. If I'm stuck and I believe my feelings are interfering in our friendship, I would get permission from you to discuss my difficult feelings, both of us knowing that the origins of those feelings are probably from the past... that it's not just about you. As I do, I would remind you that the purpose of our conversation is to get me out of my negativity, to move me forward somehow.

SANDY: We are at the point in our friendship that we can be direct with each other.

WENDY: There is a finger pricking blood pact that we have to talk to each other. We both want to make the first move in making sure our friendship is okay- it's a positive competition.

SANDY: I'm thinking our readers are probably saying, that is so... what's the word? Weird, undoable, unrealistic... too much.

WENDY: Seriously, there is no way we would ever *not* figure out a way to forgive or accept each other. Any hurts are addressed with great empathy for ourselves and for the other. What a feeling to know we will "never ever *not* get back together." (Thank you, Taylor Swift).

Takeaway

- Envy, competition and jealousy are natural emotions which can be challenging to turn into motivating forces.
- Experiencing emotions that feel "dark" at first can enrich our lives by pushing us to clarify and perhaps act on what's important to us.
- Permission, humor and play are good ways to get a difficult conversation started.

5

BRING IT HOME--Make sure there is a GOOD MOTHER in residence

WENDY: I WATCHED my mother and my older sisters so I knew as did you, Sandy, what a **good** **mother** was in the literal sense. But here we use it as a psychological term to describe aspects of an idealized person who consistently and reliably has your back in a caretaking kind of way, who wishes the best for you and would do anything to help you - as our mothers once did.

SANDY: It's a shorthand way of talking about being good to one another and, of course, to ourselves. We know that it's important to have grown up around people who loved us and valued us, because that feeling becomes incorporated into our self-confidence. We like to think of this as having a good mother *inside* ourselves.

WENDY: It's like a voice inside which might say, as an example, *"I know I'm smart and I'm loveable. I can handle this argument with my boss. And if it doesn't go well, I'll share my situation with people who know and value me and I'll go back and handle it differently and better."*

SANDY: When I think about the good mothers in my own life, I'm reminded of a moving example involving my husband, Marc, who has often and long been a good mother to me. I had gone to the doctor and received some unsettling information which left me very upset. Marc was waiting for me in the car. I left the doctor's office, opened our car door, and immediately burst into tears. Marc listened with empathy and understanding and comforted me with not just his words but also his tone of voice and his body language. He didn't try to minimize the cause of my upset. He didn't try to move on before I was ready. He let me stay with my distress until I was able to put myself back together. And believe me, it took quite a while.

I wasn't used to feeling physically vulnerable and I hated the feeling. I felt incredibly anxious. As I look back on it now, Marc might have become anxious himself as he listened to me. But whatever anxiety he might have felt at the time, he didn't let that interfere with his being available to me. It's amazing how much less alone I immediately felt, how much less frightened. It was years ago and I remember the experience vividly: such a feeling of being supported and loved.

WENDY: What a touching example of having a good mother. Marc and Jim prove the good mother can be and often is a man. Listen, it's not our fault that we are referring to an esteemed psychological principle, whose name, "*good mother,*" just might sound sexist and politically incorrect.

SANDY: Yes. And note there is an important and related concept of the "good enough" mother in psychology which reminds us that human relationships, including mother-child relationships, don't need to be perfect, nor can they be...they just need to be good enough.

Fortunately, many of us have been lucky in our early life to have had one or more good mothers (and they don't have to have been mothers, or even women, and as we've said, they don't have to have been perfect, just "good enough.") These people might have been in the role of parents, siblings, grandparents, friends, neighbors, aunts and uncles, guidance counselors or teachers. You get the idea.

WENDY: Often we receive good mothering in the groups we are part of. I am pretty sure my sister Mary Ellen uses her mahjong group and Marcia her study groups as fronts for a loving group of good mothers.

I have a different kind of good mother story. It's a story of how my mother was a good mother to me; how you are a good mother to me, Sandy; and how you helped me be a good mother to myself.

When I was a senior in high school, late on a Saturday afternoon, our veterinarian called my mother and me to tell us that my much beloved dog, Kim, had died. We were devastated. The next morning, we continued to sob while sitting in our "house coats" (the 1950s version of sweatpants - which Sandy informs me is now active wear/ leggings), poring over the Sunday paper. We were looking at the ads so that we might rescue some dog "for sale" as we rescued ourselves from our grief. My mother was intent on making me feel better, as well as herself. By 10 AM we were home with a new dog.

My sisters called from college and reprimanded us for our decision. They were pretty sure we had been grieving faultily-not waiting long enough before "replacing" our beloved dog. I am not sure if Kubler-Ross had come out with her stages of grief that long ago, but my sisters had academia on their side in their pronouncements. My mother and I were miffed by the scolding. We felt both justified and ashamed of our decision, while we were comforted in the warmth of our new dog.

Do you remember? I was telling you this story, Sandy, maybe 40 years after it happened. You quickly remarked, "Oh my God." I immediately felt a big burst of familiar shame because I believed that you too thought we had mourned improperly. These feelings might have gone on ad infinitum had I not called you back to talk about my reaction.

How happy and surprised was I when you said, "Oh no! I said 'Oh my God' because I am touched by the connection that you had with your mother." You envied the mutuality of our resolution or avoidance, whatever it was, but were admiring of our bond while I was incorrectly assuming that you felt critical of me. (And maybe you felt that too, but no way were you going to admit that now after I felt so exonerated.)

You helped me to realize that I had focused on what I had "done wrong" rather than honoring how my mom and I were being good mothers to each other as well as to ourselves by getting a new dog.

SANDY: I wanted you not to see it as wrong but to appreciate the very understandable emotions which bringing home a dog satisfied. After all, you and your mother had both suffered the enormous loss of your father many years earlier. Of course, you didn't want to feel the pain of another loss. Of course, you wanted to take that pain away.

WENDY: Yes. Also, I became aware that, in the process of feeling loved and appreciated by you, I was more able to be a good mother to my sisters. By that I mean that many years after the fact, I was able to develop a more empathic and comprehensive understanding of their feelings. I felt kinder to them in my own mind. I understood that they might not have liked being left out of the family decision, not to mention they might have feared being replaceable too.

So even though the good mother has been incorporated within me from my early childhood and so it is easier, more like "maintenance" for me to be kind to myself and others much of the time, sometimes *other people's* priorities and inter-actions can overshadow mine. That's what happened here. We all need to be reminded about how to listen to ourselves with a genuine, authentic, loving voice. And you continue to do that for me, Sandy. The good mother -Sandy- is on standby.

And no! I am not going to give you, the reader, her cell phone number.

SANDY: The more you and I talk, the more I come to appreciate that when you yourself get filled up by loving good mothers in the present day, not only are you remind-ed that you are worth receiving love and interest and empa-thy for yourself, but you are also more easily able to share that love and involvement with others around you. Another point worth making: it's never too late. We can take anoth-er look at something that pained us emotionally from our pasts and understand it differently in the light of the cur-rent day. And feel better.

WENDY: So here's another example from my child-hood, one in which perhaps I went too far on the empa-thy side for another and not enough on the empathy side for myself. When I was 10, I woke up in the middle of the night in great stomach pain. I sat outside my mother's door, whimpering, until she came out in the morning to find me. I didn't want to wake her as she had to get up early in the morning to teach school. She was the sole support of our family--three girls aged 3, 5, and 7--after my father died. My mother was shocked that I didn't wake her, especially when it turned out I needed an appendectomy. It was my choice not to wake my mother. I imagine that back then I thought my mother would have been pleased that I didn't want to disrupt her needed sleep. (See the little girl patting herself on the back.) Now I can imagine that it hurt her feelings, too, that I didn't allow her to take care of me. Perhaps I missed out on making the better choice, that I should have been a good mother to myself first and perhaps it would have been better for my mother as well.

SANDY: Perhaps??

What you described is a poignant example of you not being a good-enough mother to yourself. It illustrates the distorted perspective that a little girl can have. I can imagine though that there might have been a small part of your mother which unconsciously did encourage your self-sacrifice on her behalf. After all, she had so much on her plate. So maybe you picked up on that part of her.

WENDY: I know you're right. It is important that we learn to take good care of ourselves first, not exclusively, but first. And often I have needed you, and you have needed me, to remind one another when we can't see that clearly ourselves.

Sharing our friendship with all of you, our readers, is one way of reminding you that you can co-create a loving *good mother* voice for yourself and your friend as well.

SANDY: But, you may well ask, how do we get that *voice*, the voice of the good mother, to be a central part of ourselves, so that she is the voice we hear when we are down or disappointed? *"Come to Momma."* Supposing the voice we hear is far from being positive and supportive. Supposing the voice we grew up with is critical and shaming, making us feel stupid or bad: *"How could you do that; ... you're so stupid! Don't you think before your act?"* It's very difficult to really be a good mother to yourself unless you have had ongoing experiences of someone, hopefully more than one person, being a good mother to you. You then might be used to hearing, *"You're usually thoughtful and thorough. You'll figure out what went wrong. You will work hard to prevent it from happening again."*

WENDY: You know, there are probably many ways to learn to be a good mother to yourself despite beginnings that left a lot to be desired. We see the role of friendship as being vital to the possibility of repair. Sometimes I imagine telling you a story, Sandy, that has stumped me in the present. I feel your smile and arms around me, and I can come to my senses on my own and respond in a better way for me and the other person. Other times I find that I can wait for our next "friendship appointment" where I will discuss with you how I felt and reacted. The comfort of knowing Sandy will be happy to *have me on her knee,* listening with love and skill. (Picture this: I am 5 ft. 9" and she is 5'5.)

It may seem silly, but you and I have a set of letters that cues us and calls forth that *good mother* presence for each of us. It comes from my experience teaching graduate students in social work. My students got together and coined the phrase "What Would Wendy Say"; they used the initials WWWS when they wanted to stop themselves from handling a situation reactively rather than thoughtfully. They said the initials made them pause and empathize with the client/patient who had upset them before they reacted. I think I represented a way for my students to reach for something more than they could yet be. So after all that, here we are, using my students' advice in our friendship.

SANDY: I ask myself, "What would Wendy say? (WWWS)

WENDY: I ask myself, "What would Sandy say? (WWSS)

SANDY: And so we call forth a loving, supportive presence which calms us, slows us down, and helps us remember how we want to be. Ultimately, of course, we are trying to incorporate the loving presence into ourselves. It's an *ongoing* process: we give ourselves permission to enjoy the friendship; we remind each other to add empathy; and we make each other practice, practice, practice. Voila, our regular Tuesday mornings from 9:00 to 9:30.

WENDY: Yes. Neither rain nor snow, only broken telephone wires can stop us.

SANDY: You mean cell towers, Wendy!

WENDY: When we started, there were telephone wires.

SANDY: No, if we are being accurate, it was probably the pony express.

WENDY: Anyone who doesn't know what that is probably doesn't know "I'll have what she's having" either, and that is much more important. (Look it up, it's worth knowing.)

SANDY: I couldn't agree more!

WENDY: Seriously, let me add a word of caution. In my case, Jim thinks he is my good mother, and he is. He wants credit and he deserves it for being my mainstay. At the same time, I have worked hard to let him see how you, Sandy, *add* to our "us"; you don't *threaten* us.

We don't need just one *good mother*. And although adding a new person in our lives can expand us in positive ways, our families may not share this thought, especially in the beginning. We certainly need empathy and patience for them as they adjust to the idea of the value of friendship.

SANDY: Yes, sharing a special relationship can be challenging. It's like when a pregnant mother says to her still only child, "Guess what! We're going to bring someone else into the family to love besides you and now we're all going to share our love with the adorable new baby. Aren't you lucky!"

WENDY: Yes. Take a moment, especially if you are an only child, to imagine how that feels. Probably something like you telling your husband you are bringing home another man to live with you to share your joys...

SANDY: You and I are both incredibly fortunate to be in close, deep relationships with family members and other friends. We have a unique relationship with one another but we don't go it alone. Speaking for myself, sometimes I cannot imagine what I would do without any one of my central people: Marc, my children, my mother, my siblings and their families, my friends - they are part of my daily life in ways that keep me centered and supported and happy. Good mothers all around me.

WENDY: Wait...what about my list of good mothers? Oh, wait, I won't write mine... it's like yours but it's longer than yours and it's not a good idea to make you feel bad before we finish the book.

SANDY: Do you really think I'm going to comment after that remark? Hurry, let's go to the next chapter before you have a comeback ready for me.

Takeaway

- Take time and learn the skills to be a *good mother* to yourself and one another. Maintain a supportive, loving voice as your *self-talk* and then in your interactions, a voice that reminds you of your worth and lovability.
- One way to develop that internal voice is by using the "What Would Sandy/Wendy Say" technique, using your own friend's name.
- Practice that good mother voice by using it regularly and often. Build up that self-love/empathy *muscle*. (You should see ours! Hoping the competition keeps you pumped.)

6

STAYING OPEN-MINDED
and OPEN-HEARTED

SANDY: WENDY, YOU and I have learned that our friend-ship can enliven and foster a well-lived life, particularly when we embrace attitudes of open-mindedness and open-heartedness as ever-present mantras. Our friendship *matters*. And the *matters* of our friendship include our practice of staying open, together.

WENDY: The more open we are **in** the world and **to** the world, the happier we feel. We speak to each other on a regular basis. Our ongoing exchange is a pleasure in its own right. But in addition, we use it to keep us in shape by reminding one another to stay open to ourselves, to each other, and to our interactions with others. We have our unchangeable planned weekly phone calls on Tuesday morning, along with our "Help, I must speak in the next

12 hours..." messages which, just by sending, have already switched up our attitudes to more effective living. I could not be as capable alone. Nor would I want to be. Boot camp with Sandy is fun.

SANDY: It's true. It's the boot camp of our friendship to practice our specific attitudes of remaining open in the world. We hope our consciously applied attitudes will intrigue you so you'll want to acquire them, or tweak your own enlightened course. We certainly don't have the monopoly on the better path.

WENDY: But we are very sure that we are able to enhance our lives applying these successful attitudes -together. We enjoy each other as we become *kinder* and more *competent* people, relying on one another as a system of checks and balances.

SANDY: As we've noted earlier, these concepts are in simple ABC order. (Learn your abc's...just 7 of them this time.) Also, as we describe these in more detail, you will see that they typically overlap with one another. We're separating them in order to describe each more fully. In real life, you'll find they often can't be separated.

A. **Assumptions**: Don't make them without checking it out

B. **Boundaries:** Make them strong and yet flexible

C. **Criticism**: Learn to give it and receive it

D. **Differences**:   Learn to appreciate, not just tolerate them. No, really

E. **Empathy:**   Widen your lens and understand the other

F. **Forgiveness:**   Let go and move on

G. **Gratitude:**   Go for joy

A

ASSUMPTIONS
Don't make them without checking it out

SANDY: OF ALL our concepts, this has got to be the one
I refer myself to most frequently: don't make assumptions without checking! I think it's unbelievably common for me to make assumptions about why people do what they do without checking out their intentions, either by asking them directly or by considering other motives for their behavior. On the one hand, it probably makes sense to assume at times, because otherwise I'd never move forward in life. I'd be constantly doubting and checking. Yet, I can't tell you how often when I do check I find that I was wrong. *She wasn't angry at me; she was annoyed at something that had happened to her earlier in the day. He wasn't ignoring me; he was working out a problem in his head.*

This really hit home for me when a friend of mine told me the following story. Her beloved granddaughter, with whom she thought she had a very close relationship, wouldn't permit her to come up to camp on visiting day last summer. No explanation that made any real sense was given. My friend understandably felt hurt and confused but she didn't press the issue. This year she pre-empted that situation and told her granddaughter she wanted to come up for visiting day. "Okay," her granddaughter said slowly. "So why didn't you want me to come last year, and why do you still seem reluctant today?" my friend asked. "Oh, Nana," she said, "there are a couple of girls in the bunk who have no one come to visit, and I have my parents, my brothers and sister, and you and Grandpa. I don't want those girls to feel bad, so I thought it would feel less bad for them if there were fewer people who came to visit me."

So much for assuming without checking out the realities.

WENDY: I can only imagine the heartbreak she had the previous year, feeling slighted and unimportant.

SANDY: And because she never was able to check it out properly, her suffering turned out to be for no reason at all.

WENDY: So often we make knee-jerk assumptions that are inaccurate on the negative side and subsequently harmful to our moods and relationships. It is so important that we check out these assumptions directly when we feel bad… or

at least take the time to assume the best possible interpretations of someone's actions, as in the Jewish rabbinic teaching to "*Judge others favorably.*" Ultimately if we can, we try to
draw conclusions which assume positive intentions and then
remember to verify and ask ourselves or the source to *say
more.* While we're waiting, we challenge ourselves to "widen
our lens" to include one or more benign explanations. We
are careful not to rush to take potentially slighting or hurt-
ful comments or behaviors personally. They are usually not
meant that way. And, if they are, we are still walking around
happier and not "paying forward" our misery.

SANDY: This reminds me of a time when we missed out
on the best lobster rolls in Maine because of mutual mis-
taken assumptions. I was visiting you to work on our book.
We were about halfway through at the time and had missed
a few of our mutually agreed-upon internal deadlines.

WENDY: Damn, we are disciplined. I was in the middle
of moving and you were involved in family stuff yourself
so we both felt pressured to make quick progress. We had
planned to stop on the way from the airport to our destina-
tion in Rockland, Maine to use the bathroom in beautiful
scenic Wiscasset.

SANDY: I remember that time vividly. Over the many
years of my trips to see you in Maine you had raved about
Wiscasset. It's a small town in Southeast Maine... there's
a post office, a town hall and Red's - a funky old shack

that, you've told me so many times, houses the "best lob-ster joint in the world." (And yes, I know Maine has sev-eral thousand "best" lobster joints.) We were both hungry and a little cranky from the long drive from the airport pickup.

WENDY: I wasn't cranky. (*Sandy is rolling her eyes.*) Anyway, it is always my plan, if the line isn't too long at Red's, to get on that line so we can share a lobster roll. Somehow, I *assumed* you would want me to be diligent and focused and so it seemed irresponsible to stop and wait 45 min at Red's, even though the waiting is part of the charm. Although I was lost in reverie at the image of a whole fresh lobster heaped onto the crisply toasted bun, saturated in butter, I said, "Probably we shouldn't wait," thinking that I got points for being studious about our book- but seriously who is keeping score anyway? You took my cue and *assumed* that I didn't want to wait on line at Reds. So, without check-ing in with me, you went with *your* assumption about *my* assumption and I assumed you wanted to please me. (Uh oh! that's another assumption.) Somehow we left, both of us hungry and regretful; we found that out later. That's why we both need to read this chapter twice.

SANDY: It's a funny story and true and it makes me sali-vate for that lobster roll. It also makes the point that even when we assume incorrectly, it doesn't have to be too late to clarify and then reap the *rewards of a recap.*

WENDY: So, while we had regrets about our hunger, we no longer had regrets that we hadn't shared our thoughts and desires. It also reminds us that being in a friendship is an *ongoing process*, one which requires practice and humor.

SANDY: Learning not to take things personally is an important *companion thought* to not making assumptions. It reminds me also: clarify and question, ourselves and others, before - and after -we assume. And remember, it's not usually about you.

WENDY: Even in our 40-year post-mortem of the dog story, where my mother and I got a new dog the day after the old one died, I *assumed* my sisters had only felt critical. If we had talked it through more, I might have learned that they had many other feelings which contributed to the critical part. For example, maybe they didn't like not being included in the decision- it was their dog, too. They were sad from far away, and maybe at some level they thought if we'd get a new dog so quickly, we could probably replace a sister as well.

I think we've come to see that one way to remain open in our lives is to make our "default" perspectives as optimistic and specific as possible and to help one another do that. If we don't have the time or the will to clarify what another person's behavior means directly with that person, our goal is to *choose* our perspective. And why not make it positive?

Instead of assuming we are snubbed, consider other alternatives, e.g. whether the person is preoccupied. When we sense aloofness in a loved one's voice, let's *wonder* what is bothering them rather than assume it is about us, easy as that might be. You and I try to help one another do that. We remind each other to ask rather than be defensive or offended.

SANDY: I want to be positive, yes, but sometimes I think you can be unrealistic in how quickly you want to get to the positive. (We're different in that way.) And trying to reframe another person's behavior is not easy. Sometimes, Wendy, I think we might give that impression. It takes so much practice and reminding one another. Practice is surely the familiar refrain of this book, isn't it?

WENDY: Of course you're right. It's hard, but worth the effort to step back and consider that all of us have so many times in life that we may be overwhelmed - young children, work, breakups, kids going off to college, sickness, aging- and hence less sensitive to our impact on others. Inadvertently we may neglect or offend each other. Still, isn't it better when our grown children don't call as frequently as we would like, that we try to help ourselves and one another by reframing: imagining they are busy or having fun in their lives, or perhaps they are worried about something and could use a phone call from us. With this kindness towards them and ourselves in mind, we will try to make the phone call to them with love rather than anger or guilt-inducing behavior.

Takeaway

- Don't make assumptions. Check out assumptions directly when you can because we're so often wrong about them.
- Ask, because it increases intimacy to have those conversations.
- You can, of course, keep the assumptions that are positive or empathic and leave us feeling a rosy glow about life. (*Judge to the good...*)

SANDY: Disclaimer: that last line is from the ever-positive Wendy.

B

BOUNDARIES
Make them strong and flexible

SANDY: ONE OF the most important perspectives on life that you and I talk about, Wendy, is awareness of the importance of having strong yet flexible boundaries between ourselves and others. And by boundaries, we mean the invisible *fence* around ourselves that allows us to remember who we are, what we want and don't want, even in the presence of someone else wanting something different.

WENDY: It's the reason I like slamming doors sometimes. I remember I can have my own space and I don't have to take on the feelings of others.

SANDY: Since the cutting of umbilical cords, we struggle with maintaining the right *balance* in how we relate to others: between independence and involvement; between attachment and distance; between autonomy and intimacy; between being involved and not taking over; and between pleasing others and pleasing ourselves.

WENDY: Oh, you were supposed to cut the umbilical cord? Seriously, to maintain a healthy boundary between ourselves and another person, we need to pause and make a point of not reacting to their behavior automatically. I started out as a kid who watched my mother like a hawk, assuming I was the *cause* of any bad mood she displayed. Certainly, I felt I had to be the "fixer" of that bad mood. (Two full-time jobs for a 4-year-old.) Clearly, I felt over involved with the cause of and the cure for my mother's discomfort. Realizing I had and have a long way to go in the correction process of identifying healthy boundaries, I need concrete reminders to stay away from over involvement.

When I run into situations like these, with myself or with my patients, I have a technique that I use. I imagine Wonder Woman and her bracelets which protect her from invasion or enemy fire while she remains composed and beautiful. I too wear bracelets as she does. (That may be the end of the similarity.) Sometimes I just use the visualization technique of seeing her and her bracelets. They symbolize boundaries and choice to me.

I wear costume jewelry every day and my collection has dwindled through the years as I dispense it to patients who need something concrete to take home with them. I want the bracelets to remind them to *take a break* and not enmesh themselves with others moods, demands, or obligations without pausing to make the *choice to do so*. The "real" men in my practice have taken home some bracelets, too, and so far, no wife has questioned what it is doing in their briefcase. (Note to self: find a gender equivalent for Wonder Woman to avoid unnecessary complications.)

SANDY: I love that image of Wonder Woman! You know I always laugh when I remember one striking example of a difficulty I had with boundaries. It was many years ago, at the time when door-to-door salesmen came by selling vacuum cleaners or encyclopedias (remember those?) or whatever. In those days, I was so afraid that if I opened the door and let them in, I would be unable to say no and would end up buying at least one vacuum cleaner. My only option was to not open the door at all. I simply pretended I wasn't at home. Talk about not having flexible boundaries: I couldn't trust my ability to say no to someone who wanted something from me.

WENDY: If I was in it with you back then, you know what I'd say. I'd tell you that you don't have to choose detachment or avoidance when your boundary is tested. *Saying no with kindness* for the other's efforts or needs is sufficient. It is a skill worth practicing: *"Thank you for taking the time (sharing your thoughts, etc.) I am not going to buy that right now. You made a wonderful presentation."* The first thought you share begins with finding a *truthful, authentic, and positive* reaction which gives something in addition to your "no," but not your mood, soul, or pocketbook.

So Sandy, how many boxes of Girl Scout cookies do you have stored in your house? And you probably avoid the supermarket on the days Girl Scouts are in front with their cute little table, or perhaps you, being enterprising, call the store to find out their hours... the Girl Scouts' hours.

SANDY: Wendy, you know I adore Thin Mints, those yummy Girl Scout cookies. And I actually do have a year's supply stashed away. I've loaded your car with a few cartons; I thought you'd enjoy them.

Moving right along. You know, emotional doors are much more difficult to close than the door to my salesman. With the people closest to us, it's very easy to feel their feelings and lose our own sense of separateness. If you feel someone close to you is depressed, it's easy to absorb his or her depression (which could include wondering what you did to cause it.) If the person is anxious, it's easy to absorb the anxiety. When either of my grown children seem upset I often feel upset myself. While this may be understandable as an initial reaction, it is not helpful to anyone-neither the children nor myself-to hold this as an *ongoing* state of mind.

WENDY: Empathy is good, but getting over involved or enmeshed in their feelings is not. Sometimes people need to know they can tell you something without your day being ruined too. You don't need to take over their suffering or feel responsible for causing it or repairing it. That way they don't feel they burden you and are more free to share.

Fortunately, you only have to be in charge of one life.

SANDY: I think the issue of having good boundaries between ourselves comes up in our ukulele story. We watched ourselves change as we began with our firm positions and then discussed our opposing feelings with one another. I went from a rigid impermeable place-- *"Don't send me that ukulele!"* --to, I think, a greater openness about the possibility of accepting it. And it was based on coming to appreciate what sending the ukulele meant to you, for yourself and for me.

WENDY: I went from the more fluid boundary assumption that *everyone* loves a gift and certainly would be happy receiving it. I came to understand that gifts can feel burdensome to some people and that my impulsive generosity may backfire by feeling intrusive, as if I am pushing through boundaries uninvited.

SANDY: You know it is a lifelong human struggle to find the right space between closeness and distance, between pleasing another and pleasing ourselves. And it can change between the same people over time.

WENDY: I agree. This reminds me...when I was a young single woman and my niece was in her teens, we both enjoyed the no-boundary experience of calls at all times of the night. When I got married she was shocked, and truthfully so was I, at *our* (actually *his*, soon to be *our*, new marriage policy: no calls before 10 am or after 10 pm.) While the new policy probably horrified my niece (and me, which is another story with lots of guilt and conversation but a happy ending), my purpose was never for her to feel bad. Looking back, I hope I gave her enough affection and support for the change. The point is being able to hold on to who you are while being aware that, especially if you are doing something that you haven't done before, the other person may feel slighted or abandoned and needs your empathy, interest, and patience.

SANDY: So, we want our boundaries to be sensitive and flexible. If we are too rigid, we may be so busy protecting our independence that we won't allow ourselves to be open to another person's genuine needs and wants. On the other hand, if we are too loose with our boundaries, we may be so over involved with pleasing another person that we can lose sight of knowing what we ourselves want.

WENDY: Remember the time I had a medical test and needed a ride? I took a cab both ways instead of asking Jim to change his golf plans because I didn't want my needs to impose on his pleasure.

SANDY: Stop! I remember how upset I was with you at that time. You didn't hold onto yourself there. Going for a medical test is not something you want to do alone. And at the same time you didn't really hold on to what Jim would think was good for himself, how he'd want to be a good partner to you.

WENDY: I know! I know! I never stopped to think about how Jim would feel about not going to the proce-dure with me. I just put my own "default" need on it--not to impose- and disregarded Jim's - and mine, if I truly let myself think about what I would wish for. In fact, af-terward, Jim told me (surprise, surprise) that he was of-fended that I had not asked him to accompany me. And I myself would have been comforted by his presence. Hmmm.

SANDY: And what have we learned from this?

WENDY: That I still need a lot of coaching. That sto-ry sounded much like my past position with my mom. We bring our pasts with us, for better or for worse, don't we? Seriously, we should stay cognizant of repeating our habits from the past that, while they may have served a purpose then, don't need to be continued in the present. And that's one of the beauties of a friendship, to have that friend hold the stories of the past which need mindful correcting and updating.

SANDY: And you know what else I'm reminded of? How important it is to keep talking and to have patience with one another when we find it difficult to change.

WENDY: Yes. We have to *consciously choose* to use our friendship. This way we are free to walk away from situations enlightened instead of, as in this case, lonely, martyred, and unnecessarily repeating patterns that hurt both people.

And we don't have to get it right the first time. (We couldn't even if we tried.) There was something very satisfying for me in going back to Jim after you and I spoke. That became an intimacy in its own right.

How can we make it a habit to make these good choices? Maybe a spot check before or after you take your vitamins?

You don't have to like my jokes. I am not taking them out. That's how impermeable my humor is.

SANDY: Loosen those boundaries, honey.

Takeaway

- Keep your boundaries strong and yet flexible so you understand that another person's needs do not necessarily have to be about or involve you.
- Blurred boundaries may lead you to take over someone else's issue as your own, or to give up your autonomy.
- Healthy boundaries allow you to be involved and close and yet able to learn to say no.

C

CRITICISM
Learn to Give and to Receive it

SANDY: WELL, THIS is going to be a real challenge: staying open in the face of criticism, not to mention regulating our emotions so we can stay empathic while giving and receiving criticism.

WENDY: It reminds me of the time 25 years ago when I took my first job in Maine. My challenge was to lead a group of patients with chronic illness - to help them accept their illness and increase adherence to the overwhelming demands on their lives. This situation occurred soon after I married Jim and moved from Miami to join him in Maine. Before I left for my first day of work, Jim gave me a pep talk on appreciating the differences between down-home Maine and glittering Miami Beach. He suggested I wear less makeup and be less direct. In other words, he cautioned me to tone it down. I know he wanted the best for me.

Note to self: Remind people in my world to tell me first what is good about me as they critique me, or offer suggestions, especially where I feel vulnerable. That's part of the art of giving criticism effectively.

At the end of the group session, one of the patients said, "I have had a lot of therapists. You have been too persistent and blunt. I don't think I will come back to the group next week." I reddened, remembering Jim's words, and while I felt like slipping underneath the table, I had to concentrate on not letting any hurts get in the way of being a good professional with a healthy boundary. I spoke truthfully, one of the truths, anyway. I had to dig a bit deep to get there- searching for the positive reframe of the criticism she gave me. "I am so impressed that you could tell us what didn't work for you instead of secretly choosing not to come back. You have shown leadership in being courageous to say what you need. When you come back next week, let's make this group successful for you. I imagine others in this group will benefit from your speaking up."

I won't bore you with the rest. But when I got home, Jim, in his *good mother* way, predictably comforted me warmly and lovingly... along with subtle strains of *I told you so.* (Actually, maybe that was what I assumed he felt.) I was humbled to the quick and thought about changing careers. Two people had critiqued my style and it felt bad, very bad. I was in a funk.

Imagine my surprise when an hour later, the patient called back and said, "Dr. Rapaport, thank you. I am a bully and you tolerated me and honored my expression. I am excited to work with you." Poof! My self-esteem was back. (Seriously, how could I lose my sense of self so quickly, and yet thankfully so tentatively.)

SANDY: *Ouch!* and *Wow!* "Ouch" because I am *naming* what I feel when I empathize with you, criticism stings, and "Wow" because I am impressed with how well you handled yourself. You had the presence of mind and heart to respond very effectively to that group member. And you started out in such a vulnerable situation, working in a new community with a different set of norms, and feeling somewhat unsure after being warned by Jim. You tolerated criticism without being defensive and at the same time really listened to what the other had to say. And it worked… for all of you.

WENDY: I love *Ouch and Wow.* To me it's a wonderful cue for recognizing that something hurt me with an attached reminder to *regulate* my emotions so that what I say next is more likely to satisfy me and the other person, wowing us both. I am going to use it. My poor patients are going to come out singing *Ouch and Wow,* too.

SANDY: I'm not so sure that I'll be using it. I can definitely feel the controlled sting of saying *Ouch,* but I'm not sure I can rise to doing a *Wow.* We'll see.

The *Ouch* is usually going to be there though, isn't it? Nobody likes criticism, implicit or direct. Even if it's well-founded (maybe especially if it's well-founded), even if it's gently given, it doesn't feel good to most of us, at least at first. Sometimes I think most of us are made of such sensitive mush inside that it takes very little to penetrate our exterior and wound that vulnerable inside. That's why I'm so impressed with your handling of this. You didn't retaliate, even subtly; you just listened and tolerated the criticism, perhaps intuitively knowing the patient was possibly talking about herself and her own issues...

WENDY: Yes, and although her comment was about me, it was just her experience of me - which doesn't make it true in general, just her opinion. I don't have to fall apart at someone's opinion.

SANDY: I can hear the *good mother* place in your secure self from which you could think that through to manage your hurt.

WENDY: Yes, I had to pause and muster every bit of empathy in range. In this case, I did believe it was not about me; she was letting me know about her, that she was critical and blunt with others. If I had not heard her and was instead defensive or aggressive, I would have missed being able to help her out of her pain. This underscores what we need in our professional and personal lives. Thank goodness I had you speaking to me twice a week during my transition to moving to Maine.

SANDY: I was trying to think of an example between you and me, Wendy, and couldn't easily come up with one. Do we never dare criticize one another? Do we never have anything to criticize? None of that can be true. I think we are very careful in presenting our complaints to one another and it is softened by a backdrop of feeling loved so it hurts less.

WENDY: I think when we *give criticisms* to each other, it's a good thing to alert the person that we have something difficult to say or even get permission to talk about it. We artfully and accurately give empathy and perspective to each other, first, in order for us to highlight perspective of our whole picture. Then we include what we would want- not just what has upset us, so we have allowed for the *possibility* of making changes.

When I used to come to New York to visit my sisters and didn't see you, you might have said, "You selfish #@$%&." Instead, you were gracious about telling me first how much you admired my close relationships with my family in New York when I visited them. Then you reminded me that I could make room for you, too, when I came to the city, and asked me to make a specific plan to meet you. Truth is, you gave me the courage and clarity to expand my overly loyal boundaries and my sisters probably thank you for taking me off their backs.

SANDY: Maybe the too-much-told story of the ukulele can also serve to illustrate this. I felt criticized, however gently, by you because I didn't want you to give me the present and I felt pressured by your persistence despite my expressed reluctance. You thought I was wrong not to take it. I felt annoyed. But we stayed open, saying *Tell me more* to each other, which didn't mean we agreed but we were willing to listen with an open mind. (Take a moment to visualize the clenched jaw and tightened gut ... just below the surface.)

WENDY: And I felt ashamed about my OCD (*obsessive caring disorder*) and impulsivity. But because the unstated criticism was at the same time an opening to *self-reflection* on *both* of our parts, neither of us was the "bad" one. We each took responsibility for the emotions we felt so our annoyed emotions disappeared pretty quickly. (I think yours did as well. Uh oh-assumption.) The good part was that each of us could see and decide if we were willing to modify our reactions. If we did not, neither was going to be self righteous about our correctness. We were different. Period.

SANDY: You know, Wendy, most of us are not going to go through the slow motion process that you and I went through here.

WENDY: It is a good idea, however, to do it with important people and difficult situations. It takes practice and commitment to master these behaviors. They don't come naturally. We need to remind ourselves to use the following *skills,* with authenticity: the skill of **"Naming"** (giving a description of what you see or feel, e.g. *"Ouch");* **Clarification** by saying *Tell me more;* and **Positive Reframing,** highlighting the positive of a situation, as I did with my first patient in Bangor. It's core training for the mind.

SANDY: Yes, and as a reminder to ourselves, you and I slow ourselves down in part because we are self-observant, especially while we're writing this book, but also because that is our *process.* This is what we do. I know it's something everyone can begin to learn if they are motivated. Slowing down always seems like the first step. When someone criticizes me, I take a deep breath and try not to let my hurt feelings cause me to react right away.

WENDY: I agree. But where we very much need one another's loving support is at the next step: to be able to look at which parts of the criticism make sense to us and which parts don't. When we ask for *Clarification,* that genuinely validates the other person. At the same time, we try to understand what the other person is criticizing before we let it penetrate. You and I try to help one another with this.

SANDY: Often a criticism is totally unfounded. Maybe the person criticizing you is in a bad mood, having been criticized herself earlier, and takes it out on you. That can be so painful. Maybe the critic is frequently critical; particularly in that case you should not take it personally. Worse still is when you or a critic includes those dangerous words *always* or *never* in the criticism. We keep trying to learn to thicken our skins so that the misplaced wounding words are not allowed to penetrate.

WENDY: But if it's a valid criticism, it's important to let it pass through. If this criticism feels dangerous to your self-esteem, this is where I especially want to be by your side by reminding you that this criticism is not about your entire character. That is, this is not going global; your value as a human being remains intact even if you have disappointed someone or angered them. (Can you hear *good mother?*) And you are still lovable. (Repeat after me.) We are there to remind one another of that. And when we can, we *ask permission* of each other, e.g. "I need to say something difficult. Is this a good time?"

And, of course, we try to listen to any anger that might come back, still holding the ability to stay with what needs to be said, *with compassion.*

SANDY: Wendy, give me a break. That's way too much control and compassion for me to expect of myself. And it sounds like every conversation becomes a teaching moment. I don't want to do that all the time. And I don't think others want to hear it all the time.

WENDY: Okay. Okay. Sandy, you are older than I am (one day). Maybe the age difference has made you more vulnerable to burnout. You should read this chapter more often.

SANDY: Enough of this mindful compassion and maturity! Let's take this outside.

WENDY: Sandy is lying face down in the ground.

SANDY: You wish.

WENDY: But seriously, I do hear the criticism. I make way too many training opportunities. (My sisters are smiling broadly and thanking you...you let the goody-goody teacher have it.)

SANDY: Can't I ever have the last word!

Takeaway

- When taking in criticism, use *Ouch and Wow,* your new best friends. This is the skill of **Naming**, of observing and describing the facts and your feelings. This is followed by steadying yourself so you can keep your cool when you respond.
- As we give or take in criticism, carefully, use the skill of **Clarification** and say "Tell me more." Tolerate the sting and then try to understand it. Throw away the parts that don't fit.
- When giving criticism: Take the good mother stance, and authentically try to remember and share the good (for perspective sake) by using the skill of **Positive Reframing** -as well as what *specifically* hurts or what you need from the other person. In this way the *opportunity* for satisfaction is built into the criticism.

D

DIFFERENCES
Appreciate them. No, really.

WENDY: YOU KNOW what I love? When my husband squeezes my hand while we're in the movies at the part we both get excited about, or when we 100% agree that we liked it. I adore thinking we have exactly the same taste. When we are the same, I feel safe, as if all is right in the world--that I am correct in my perceptions and I am not alone.

SANDY: Excuse me, how old did you say you were? On the other hand, I have to admit, I know what you mean. It does feel good to be joined by another in opinions, wishes, ideas. It is a normal human feeling to want to be part of the in-group, to want to belong.

Conversely, it's not easy to appreciate people who have different views, opinions, or desires from our own. It's not easy to truly appreciate difference, the "other," everyone who is "not me." And I mean appreciate, not just tolerate.

I might have one view on abortion and someone I like might have an opposing one. If I respect that person, I want to try to remain genuinely open and curious about how she arrived at her position. I want to hold back from feeling criticism, especially condescension. I don't have to end up agreeing, certainly, but I want to aim to be open to understanding. It's another way in which empathy is involved. Trying to put yourself into the other person's mind and heart. On purpose.

WENDY: You are talking about deliberately having a lot of self control in order to find the empathy.

SANDY: Yes. It's about trying to stay genuinely curious and open.

I was wondering about that desire you express to share Jim's likes and opinions. I think that it starts very early in life, that feeling of wanting to be like the other. We and our mommies were one to begin with. Our survival and well-being depended on her. It takes years of development to begin to be separate (beginning with those "terrible twos") and at the same time maintain a feeling of connection. It's a delicate balance.

WENDY: It seems more reasonable when I was seven to be thrilled that my best friend's favorite color was also blue or that we both ate the black jelly beans, even though we didn't like them, for fear of hurting *someone's* feelings.

I have trained myself to pass through the insecure feeling I get when I first discover differences between me and a close friend or colleague. In a "180" I look up with eagerness -that's a stretch- to hear the contrast and want to know it, understand it, take in the parts that make sense, and respect the perspective of the "other." While I still initially recoil, I remind myself it certainly doesn't mean my perspective is wrong. At the same time, it doesn't mean I am right. And, actually, it could be an opportunity to learn something new.

SANDY: We both recognize that experiencing difference from someone we're very connected to evokes feelings. For some, it feels bad and lonely, like being adrift in too much separateness, too big a boundary. For some it feels freeing, like enough individuality is permitted. You're saying you tend to come from a place where you're learning to tolerate and not just tolerate but actually appreciate difference.

WENDY: Right. It is sometimes not easy to hold on to my individuality and stay with respecting *my* difference and the *other* person's difference, as well. In this example, (my initial reaction is not typical, but it can happen like this), Jim and I are at a dinner party. The wine and conversation flows; the banter is fervent about current events, feminism, equal rights. Jim, a quietly funny man, squeezes my hand as my laughter and conversation turn somewhere between vibrant and raucous. Immediately, I feel reprimanded and shamed. My face burns with embarrassment; I am too loud for him, I think. Without conversation or self-regulation, my shame could erode to isolation and anger and we'd both be entering the fight club for the rest of the night.

SANDY: Wendy, how quickly you interpreted his squeezing your hand as thinking you need to change, that there is only one right way to be at a party. BTW, are you ever not holding Jim's hand? Seriously, look at how you experienced Jim's squeezing your hand differently in the two examples you just described. First, you love the feeling of connection that flows between you through your hands and now you feel chastised by him. You can see the power and danger of *assuming* ... there are so many possible interpretations.

WENDY: Yes. Somehow at this dinner party I initially interpreted his clutch of my hand as a cue to alter my behavior. When I took the time to reflect, I was able to interpret that same clutch as possibly his desire for connection with me. Now that's using the skill of a *Positive Reframe*, seeing the situation in a more positive light, for him and me. And, after more thought, I could be more sensitive to Jim as an introvert needing a push by an extrovert to be invited in; he might be requesting that I involve him in the conversation. If in fact it was truly disapproval, how is it that I would let one beloved and gentle man's shy nature suggest I change my socialization style? Why wouldn't I just tolerate that he might have a different style than I do or a different need, not better or worse, just different?

I can see it is about me, not him. I didn't have to be angry and I didn't have to change, either.

Look at all the work I did on a squeezing of the hand.

SANDY: I see that it doesn't have to be either/or. We can be so programmed from our past relationships and our wish to be pleasing to those we love. It's often hard to remind ourselves that we don't have to be clones of one another. That's the good news.

WENDY: If I receive criticism from Jim for an area of our difference--for example, if I learn that he did wish that I wasn't as gregarious as I was--then I want to be able to honestly and warmly say, "Tell me more about what bothers you. I'm happily me although I am always interested in what you have to say. And, certainly, I want you to be comfortable, too."

SANDY: And I want us to learn to seriously appreciate difference as a good, not just as something to tolerate.

WENDY: This is true for us, Sandy. We describe our differences with alternative explanations rather than judgment. I actually can't wait to talk to you because I value the differences in how each of us thinks. I know when I call you, I need to change gears. Your responses often involve slowing down, being less reactive, going deeper rather than wider.

SANDY: One of the values for me in writing this book has been to come to appreciate our differences. I see you as much more of an activist than I am and the book is filled with your wise interventions.

WENDY: You mean my impulsive/spontaneous movements? *Let's do this...*

SANDY: STOP. I haven't finished my thoughts yet. It hasn't always been easy for me to appreciate that about you in writing the book because your inclinations and mine are so different. I tend to be more passive.

WENDY: Not passive - thoughtful... really listening.

SANDY: Ok. I like that. So, as I was saying, I tend to listen and wait and not give advice. I guess because I hate being told what to do, I don't like to tell others. But because we have spent so many hours writing this opus and having to incorporate both worldviews, I did end up recognizing that much of the time, maybe most, people can grow from thoughtful interventions. I've come to appreciate your style and accept that I'm not going to *be* you or like you in that way. I admire you and accept that we are not the same. I want you to hold on to being you and me to being me.

WENDY: The greatness of you is how you listen and ask questions first, a beautiful gift to let others figure out what they need or even wait to let them ask for it. I do know my strengths, but you have added a significant growth in how I respond ...*WWSS*... *What Would Sandy Say.* It often translates as pausing and asking for more from the other. I have enjoyed that in you so much. Your process is actually validating to me- that my thoughts matter, and that you want to know more. And that makes me think I have the capability to come up with my own answers.

Let me add a point: We must appreciate deeply the differences between men and women, remaining respectful and not stereotyping as we do this. For many men, their success is measured by going for the bottom line, making decisions, and getting the job done. Many women require another dimension, *connection*. For women, the relating is as important as obtaining the goal, and may in fact be the goal. Men and women need patience with each other for their differently prioritized objectives. I guess I'm hoping that in addition to having awareness of personality differences, women and men recognize and inform or "teach" their differing needs with compassion to each other so they both expand their repertoire of skill and style.

SANDY: You know, Wendy, that Marc and I reflect gender differences as well as personality differences in ways that I think are pretty common. We say to each other that we have different rhythms. Marc is a great planner, way ahead of me in anticipating, way ahead of me in organizing. He is chief of financial planning and vacation planning and so much else that I value and admire. I used to feel annoyed with him for taking over, and annoyed with myself for feeling less than competent as, less than powerful as, he seemed. Now I have truly learned to appreciate our differences. Perhaps I'm better at making and keeping personal relationships going. We all can't do it all. So now I experience us as a team working together, with different and complementary strengths and weaknesses. At the same time, I do believe we've grown from each other and have incorporated aspects of one another in ourselves. I still rely on him to make the plane reservations, though, and I love being able to!

WENDY: This is our last weekend (really?) writing *Friendship Matters*. We are determined to spend the entire weekend, each in our own home, in boot camp style. The rules are: no malingering in the bathroom; not too many carbohydrates at lunch so we stay alert; and no wine before 5. (I had tried to push the last one back to 3:30.) We are laughing and talking and writing and miraculously our bladders are in sync and we are taking our bathroom breaks together.

SANDY: Those in-sync bathroom breaks remind me of our first meeting. Only now, 45 years later, instead of talking, we are texting each other while peeing.

WENDY: I am wearing long earrings and an Indian shirt, remnants of my hippie days. I have makeup on, thick black eyeliner and red lipstick and nail polish, even though we are staying home all day and it's 8:45 AM on a Saturday. I am imagining your sparkling blue eyes and flawless skin and forever the trim figure, rolling out of bed and easily looking stunning in your sweatpants...a natural beauty.

SANDY: Thank heavens there is no verification of this through Face Time or Skype. It's a delicious fantasy and I'm going with it!

If only our readers could see us now, Wendy. You quickly and wittily writing your response before I've even had a chance to formulate my words! We're like dueling computers, only occasionally sitting next to each other in *real life*, but always sitting in front of my Mac and your PC.

WENDY: You can tell by the name brands that Sandy is more sophisticated than I am.

SANDY: Stop interrupting! We are sharing the same online draft of our book, and having a conversation through our fingers on the keyboard. Sometimes it seems to happen faster than a spoken conversation. OMG, it's happening now, even as I'm typing this you're ahead of me writing something that I'm going to be jealous of, because it's clever and funny and…. Wait up!!!!

Takeaway

- It's human nature to want to seek similarities between yourself and others.
- At the same time, it's important to hold onto your individuality as you remain open to appreciating and learning from the differences between yourself and friends.
- Respecting differences can expand you, sharpening or adding to your outlook and skills.

E

EMPATHY
Widen your lens and understand
the other person

WENDY: IT'S B-A-A-A-A-CK...COMPLEXITY, perspective...*it's not just about you.*

SANDY: Wendy, here is a story from the early years of my marriage. My mother-in-law, after my husband and I would visit from our home about an hour away, always wanted us to call her as soon as we arrived home. At that time I experienced her behavior as controlling and negative. (You, our astute readers, probably recognize my issues already.) Anyway, I bristled at having to call her. I remember telling you and expecting sympathy.

WENDY: And in retrospect, I wish I had given you more *validation* for your reaction first before I asked you to "widen your lens" with empathy and enter a more compassionate mode for her, as well as you. (And while I am at it, can I collectively apologize to everyone else I didn't support in that way, first.) Note, by validation, I mean the skill of listening to and honoring someone else's perspective. (E.g., "I get you.") It does not require agreement, but it confirms that you are wanting to see and know their experience. It strengthens your relationships.

SANDY: It was helpful that you told me to think of other reasons for my mother-in-law's desire for the phone call. You suggested that it could be experienced as a reflection of caring, not of control. (Positive Reframing.) For a woman who didn't drive distances, an hour's drive could feel anxiety-provoking, much like I might today experience my grown children's plane flight to another part of the world. Wow! That's a more helpful explanation, I thought. And it helped. My mother-in-law's anxiety didn't have to be passed onto me (thank you, boundaries), just understood in the same way that I try not to add to my children's anxiety when I am concerned. (Hmmm, maybe because I don't ask my children to call, they just think I don't care at all. Is there no right way?)

WENDY: Another reason it's good that you found ways to not stay angry at her is because it might have complicated your relationship with Marc, her son. He would have unnecessarily been put in the middle.

SANDY: Sigh. Old fashioned empathy and compassion work wonders for loosening our grip on feeling annoyed, ashamed, or criticized. This can change our moods and our relationships.

Yes, empathy is back! On our pages, but perhaps not enough in the world's conversations. (Don't let me get started on that...) Earlier in the book, we talked about empathy as a basic skill of *emotional literacy,* especially our ability to see the world with nuance. It seems to us to be significant enough to devote a specific chapter to describing it more fully. Empathy underpins everything for us, especially our ability to understand the world as complex, with many valid points of view, even though they may differ from each other. When we look at life, we try to resist the temptation to see any issue as black or white, right or wrong, or only from our perspective.

Whether it's at the global or the personal level, we try not to use a lens in which one side can be seen as totally the good guy and the other as the bad guy. Even within people, we have different aspects of ourselves. Frequently our reactions to people or events are made up of complex, often contradictory feelings. We can feel both love and anger for someone, and often at the same time.

WENDY: Empathy means I try to understand where another person comes from in thoughts, feelings, and behavior. I imagine how I might feel if I were that person. I try to understand without judgment how she got to that place. It does not mean I have to end up agreeing with her, but it does mean I want to be interested in her well-being. I think this process can bring me closer to the other person as I acknowledge her worth by listening, and my own worth by my compassion - concern and understanding. It reminds me I can *feel* hurt if someone yells at me, but not *stay* hurt, as for example if a friend offends me, I take a moment to remember she is going through a difficult divorce. I feel better by being empathic because it helps me manage my emotions and not react with anger. I save my day and perhaps I don't add to the other's stress.

SANDY: It is good to try to make a habit of being empathic if it doesn't always come naturally. We need empathy to be able to widen our lens and learn to understand someone's behavior even when it's unfamiliar and therefore uncomfortable to us. That reminds me... You knew my father, Wendy.

WENDY: Yes, he had such presence. I remember him as dynamic, tall, handsome, and strong.

SANDY: I don't want to go off topic here, but really, he was handsome, yes, but shy, so not a strong presence in a group, and of average height.

WENDY: Clearly, let's keep in mind one of our differences… as we report our truths…and that is that you are understated.

SANDY: And maybe you will own up to that not everything is beautiful, wonderful and fabulous.

WENDY: Perfectly said.

SANDY: [Groan]. Enough already. Seriously.

I want to get back to my father. He was a modest, kind, gentle man, an engineer by training but a stock market guy by interest. Actually, he was curious about all ideas. When my parents lived near Princeton, New Jersey after their retirement, he audited courses at the university in a variety of fields, from religion to history. So, when he began to suffer from dementia, it was particularly painful for all of us. As my father gradually became less and less himself and ultimately was unable to communicate with words, our family tried to find a way to reach him. All of us were loving but confused about how to connect with my father.

We wanted him to know that we loved him. My sister and I, his two daughters, were particularly invested in a purposeful attempt at empathy, an attempt which required each of us to widen our lens. We tried to imagine ourselves as him. Perhaps this mute man still had emotional awareness. What might reach him? We read to him, played music for him, sang songs to him. We came to see that family photos on the iPod evoked an emotional response from this man who treasured his family. Sometimes we thought we heard a few whispered names from him. Perhaps we did reach him.

WENDY: The conscious practice of reaching for empathy probably reduced your suffering and, as an added benefit, made you more effective. It sounds like your conversations of *expressing* the empathy to each other made your sister and you even closer. Certainly, when we express our empathy to another, the outcome often is that we feel more intimate.

By the way, your examples serve as a reminder of how long, how luckily long, we have been supporting one another. And please don't miss the point that *friendship matters,* no matter when you meet that friend. You can make an intimate friend at any time in life. It's never too late. No matter when you hear the stories that make up your pasts, they become a part of the friendship. Sometimes you forget that you weren't there in reality.

SANDY: Here's yet another example--one that goes back to our core differences in approaching life. This too is very current. You have just finished work on another book and are engaged in many emotionally draining activities, including moving. I have been working on our book and am excited because I have a new approach that I want to share with you. I hold back, not wanting to share my thoughts until you are ready (my bottom-line position: don't intrude). But you don't seem to be ready. When you do read the new work, your response, though positive, seems not as invested as you usually are. Can you imagine, you said, "That sounds nice"? From you!!! That's like saying " Bor-ing." I am disappointed but don't express it. I decide to wait until you come back to being ready, which I know will happen.

WENDY: NO! (That's me, yelling.) Not the most helpful of approaches with me. You could have just communicated your excitement about what you are writing and your eagerness for me to be ready to be involved. Without doing that, I don't know what you are thinking and feeling. I didn't "hear" you as I often might because I was in fact distracted. Feeling your desire for more immediate connection with me would probably have pushed me to get back into our book more quickly. At that point, if you had *expressed* your empathy--"Are you okay? You are not your usual responsive self" --we would have had an open conversation that satisfied us both.

Takeaway

- Work on being empathic. You can "widen your lens" to understand how others might view something - without judgment- and **validate** their experience.
- It turns out that "feeling" empathy for another can help you manage your emotions; it can be a kindness to you as well as the other person.
- *Expressing* empathy facilitates connection with others.

F

FORGIVENESS
Let go and move on

WENDY: AT ONE time or another, each of us has been rejected, insulted or hurt. What we do with those painful feelings can be our choice. We can choose to wallow in the unpleasant feelings, feeling angry and self-righteous as we hold a grudge. But we can also *choose* to forgive, to let it go and move on. Taking this higher road is not easy...but ultimately it is rewarding.

SANDY: I immediately remember an example in which I was utterly unable to get past being insulted. I did not forgive. I did not move on. It has been almost 20 years and it's only now that in talking about this issue with you, I can try to take a look, understand, let go, and at long last move on.

The story goes like this: I worked as a psychologist in the lower elementary school of a school district. I had spent nine years in that setting, and before that seven years in the high school. I loved the lower school and was considered, I believe, a valuable member of the school community. It takes years for a psychologist to become an integral member of the school family and I had achieved a place where I felt effective.

One day my supervisor asked me if I would like to leave my position and move to the middle school because they needed a strong psychologist there. I quickly said, "No way!" Several weeks later I was informed by letter that I would be reassigned that following September to the middle school. No further discussion! I was reassigned.

I can't begin to describe the enormity of my rage at my supervisor. It consumed me. After taking a few weeks to consider, I put in my resignation. I never spoke to my supervisor again. Ever. My career after the school position has been happy and fulfilling, yet I still wonder at the power of my inability to find a forgiving attitude in myself.

WENDY: Forgiving to you and to him?

SANDY: No! Forget him. Forgiving to myself.

WENDY: Uh oh. Not enough validation for your pain. I spoke too fast. It's an old story, but I still feel it fresh as we are talking.

SANDY: I moved on in my career, but not in my attitude. Why have I been so stuck?

WENDY: I can hear how powerless and invisible you felt - at the mercy of someone else controlling your life based on his needs, not your wishes. (I know that injury makes you overlook the compliment to you as to why he asked you in the first place.) You didn't actually see that it was your choice to have a forgiving attitude or perhaps even a challenging one; but yes, you could have chosen to forgive and move on if you felt that it was a viable and concrete option.

SANDY: I seriously don't get it, Wendy. How can forgiveness be viewed as an option?

WENDY: It's a point of view that you *decide* to take: I will forgive so I can find peace and not take up so much space in my life with negativity. If I can, I will find a way to make something good come out of the pain. Actually, you did use your unhappiness at your school reassignment to make something good happen for yourself, Sandy. You were able to further your career in a meaningful way; you took the pain of being vulnerable to a boss and branched out on your own, with yourself as your boss- taking an independence route which otherwise might have been difficult to initiate.

So, it's a decision to let go and move on, and that takes work. It's a purposeful process involving feeling, understanding, lots of complaining, plenty of validating and ultimately reframing. You needed to spend time to stay with your difficult feelings. Then you had to understand what feeling powerless and insignificant meant to you, why it made you so very angry, why you felt such rage at the perpetrator for being thoughtless and insensitive.

You might even have heard the compliment about your abilities.

In time, you could make a decision that you would choose to see the situation differently. And you did in your choices, if not your feeling; you used this kick in the ass to push you to move on.

SANDY: You know, some part deep within me is beginning to understand. My anger has actually receded as we revisit this. It's not all gone but I do see that my supervisor did what he thought he had to do, although he did it quite poorly. I didn't like it then and I don't like it now. But I get it. I accept the reality. He treated me shabbily and with disrespect.

But I don't want to stay stuck with this. I want to move on. And I have to work at forgiving myself for staying stuck as long as I did. As we revisit this old issue in the comfort of our friendship, our conversation amazingly helps me heal this old wound.

WENDY: It is hard at first, of course, to go the forgiving attitude route, but if we don't move past the familiar inflammatory story which can generate palpable anger and resentment, we might be telling our story for the next 20 years. Cost effectiveness- wise, forgiving is the only way to go.

Things didn't work out your way... life's not fair... it's all true... but we need to find the best ways to let go: spend time with your trusted *good mothers* to repeat the story (and bore them...thank you, that's why therapists are also great...we don't worry about boring them) ...and seriously we don't worry about boring each other. Our *good mother* connection is airtight.

Choosing a forgiving attitude takes mindful purpose and practice. Beginning with self-compassion- which I don't think we come by naturally -we can set the stage for paying it forward, to forgive others, too. In my case, I am finally able to forgive myself for not reading friends' and colleagues' books, as I see now they haven't read mine. The resistance on all our parts is complicated. The recognition of this frees me from longstanding guilt and shame for not reading others' works (Does this count as an apology?) I forgive myself. And I forgive others that they have not read mine. (And I wish they had challenged my procrastination ... perhaps I should do the same...)

Sometimes it feels like a sacrifice to forgive another; it feels unfair: *I hate being the brunt of her anger. I realize it is her mood and not about me. Why doesn't she apologize? It's not right. But I guess she can't. I will give her a pass or talk about it with her later.* Forgiving is a process that actually frees both of us. In some cases the forgiving is done all in our heads or with an empathic friend who listens and supports us.

Imagine what we can do with our time if we are not feeling angry, vengeful or self-righteous?

SANDY: Here's a smaller example of letting go and moving on. Whenever I feel at the mercy of someone who breaks the rules, unwritten or not, I feel angry and want to retaliate. I feel like I generally am a "good girl" who follows the rules so I resent when someone else chooses not to.

An everyday example: I feel road rage whenever I'm driving and someone attempts to cut into a long single line of cars trying to exit a road. I don't want to let the car into line and I don't want anyone else to either. Surely that is not the high road. Certainly, it is not good for my health either as I feel tense and annoyed and impatient and ...I could go on, but you get the idea.

WENDY: So what do you do? (I'm admitting nothing about myself here.)

SANDY: I've tried to use techniques which we've already discussed, such as widening my lens and not making assumptions. For example, I say to myself, perhaps the driver is feeling ill or has an emergency which requires immediate attention. (He is in a sports car with the top down and cool shades, but you never know...) If I knew that, I'd be incredibly happy to let the car in ahead of me. That sometimes helps. I try to distract myself with what I'm listening to, music or a book. I try to tell myself that it makes no sense to give the driver the power to ruin my own precious time, and I don't want to squander my time. It takes so much practice to remind myself that there is no point in being angry (irked, annoyed, raging - all shades of anger); it's so damaging to my attempts to maintain an inner tranquility.

WENDY: I love your clear explanation of describing awareness and skill. You have allowed yourself to have feelings of anger and revenge. Check. Now move to the upside of the dark side and use the last skill. Take the leap. Choose to take a more enlightened stance - *just because*. It's an exercise of consciously changing your beliefs because it is better for your health, your driving, your prison record, and seriously your life and the life of those around you.

SANDY: I like that: Do it just because. I want us both to learn how to soothe ourselves and one another in stressful situations. Maybe taking the high road can help. But believe me, I'm going to have to work very hard when I get in the car and face the morning traffic.

WENDY: This is not easy, but it's worth it. Changing a familiar way has powerful pulls. We use insight, challenge, and practice.

Is that a police siren I hear?

Since we are already in the car, I have another car story. Per my usual pleasant routine, I was talking to my sister and brother-in-law the other day on the phone. They have a wonderful habit of calling people they love while driving out of New York City to the country on the weekends. The speakerphone is on, and I overhear their conversation in the car: "Turn there. Don't go so fast. Your cell phone is ringing."

One *could* feel peripheral to the conversation. I always choose to feel that I like being a part of the texture of their lives. If I don't initially, I give myself a moment to feel "less than" and then decide that's a waste and rejoin the reverie.

It is easy for me to choose the positive. It is useful when I work with patients to help them expand their interpretation of situations. For example, when their grown children call them on their way home from work, I try to help them see that it is not an insult, but a compliment that the children think of them in their first free moment. (positive reframe.)

SANDY: (The Cynic) You do that? You always change the interpretation of how people behave toward you into the positive? And is that what you mean by taking the high road? Because I'm not sure I'm there and I'm not sure I want to be there.

WENDY: Yes. My mother's theology was positivity. Let's be honest, it was also denial. It was a bit extreme. She did not want to allow for any negative thoughts to enter her own consciousness.

SANDY: And how did that affect you, I ask, as I suggest the obvious. But I do believe that if, like you, someone *genuinely* holds a positive stance about life, it can make life easier and happier. If you can positively reframe people's actions or life events in a positive way, you're less disappointed and frustrated. At the same time, we have to ask what are the downsides of denial.

WENDY: One downside of denial is that no one asks me who to hire. They are pretty sure I am missing out on noticing the parts that don't work. And in my life, when I don't see things, there is no opportunity to change things. Jim may just be luckier than he realizes, seen with such positive eyes. And hey, you are pretty perfect too. I admired my mother and I am so much like her. My big change now is allowing myself to give up the denial and "see" but not stay with the negative.

SANDY: You recognize that most of us aren't coming from that place, don't you?

WENDY: I do, but stored deep in my memory bank is the experience that I always feel better when I take this position; with this knowledge of success, all I need is a gentle nudge to start the positive chain. It doesn't mean you can't nurse the hurt or anger for a sufficient time, but *really*, eventually it's time to move forward.

SANDY: Sometimes I do want to feel sorry for myself. But the truth is, that doesn't really satisfy me at the end of the day. What works best for me is asking myself if I am being the kind of person I want to be in any given situation, independent of how the other person is behaving. If I want to feel true to myself, I may have to find ways to keep the other's negativity from penetrating me.

WENDY: I too have come a long way, but from a different direction. In the past I never allowed myself to feel any annoyance at all. Now I register it. Then, I go back to trying to be positive - though sometimes it takes a small sledge hammer to move in that direction.

SANDY: Hmm. As we're coasting along our High Road Highway, I want us to remember that at times we should acknowledge and deal with the negative. Even stay there for a while. Sometimes it's not just appropriate but also useful for us to slow it down and acknowledge and stay with the negative for a time.

WENDY: Appreciating the negative is a celebration of being human. What do you think?

SANDY: I think that's an exaggeration. It's a recognition of being human, not a celebration.

WENDY: Damn. You always remind me to calm down.... Can't a kid just go off on her soapbox?

SANDY: Is that a thank you for clarifying?

Takeaway

- *Choose* a forgiving attitude.... Practice it 10,000 times and it's yours!
- Forgiveness isn't easy or instant. It's a deliberate process involving feeling, understanding, and ultimately modifying your point of view.
- You can nurture annoyance for a while, but wallowing in negativity hurts mainly you. Eventually take the high road to free yourself and others.

G

GRATITUDE
Go for joy

WENDY: *Count your blessings* still rings true. Sorry Mom for making fun of you for saying that back then. It felt simplistic and clichéd when she said it. It seemed she cut into my griping-only session way too early. The updated version of this idea has mothers telling themselves and their children to *practice gratitude.*

SANDY: Aha! Oh, so you did harbor some negative thoughts at some point in your life! I knew it! And by the way, what does that mean to you, Wendy, to *practice gratitude?* That phrase is so overused, it starts to sound trite and unexciting, don't you think?

WENDY: I think the idea of practice implies that it is not always natural and so it reminds us to create a habit. I think that when you and I talk about it, we mean a kind of daily mindfulness in which we *choose* to focus our attention on what is going well in our lives. We take time to say to ourselves what pleases us and makes us feel lucky, be it small or big things. The other aspect is sharing the gratitude with those around us. It is part of how Jim and I say goodnight. When we focus on the positives, we are on the path for joy.

SANDY: You're right. I think you and I intentionally help one another *notice* the little things in life that bring gratitude and joy: a laugh over something funny that happened to one of us; a camp song sung aloud as we kayaked together; an awareness of the beauty of a Maine sunset on the water; and in general, a deep appreciation of the wonders of life and love. We observe things and communicate our observations to each other. We feel blessed and grateful. And we have *conversations.* saying how much we appreciate each other. Often.

WENDY: We know one of the best ways to ensure joy is to **be careful who your friends are.** Our parents told us this. We didn't always respect it. (So many amends, so little time.) Seriously, it's important to always be mindful of who influences you through your lifetime and to choose carefully, not just when we're kids. As adults, the people around us still influence the way we think and the behaviors we choose.

SANDY: You and I do share the pleasure of *noticing* and *telling* each other about our *positive feelings*. It seems to me that people are always ready to share what bothers them-injuries and disappointments. Those are important, but adding balance by sharing what you like, what helped you, is equally necessary. That's the gratitude, which is an internal pleasure and, when communicated, a source of satisfaction in your relationships.

WENDY: Research says the expression of gratitude goes straight to the hypothalamus, the part of the brain associated with pleasure sensations. But, of course, if we accent what is going well, we are probably going to feel better than if we obsess on what's wrong. I like when life is simple like that.

So here's the vocabulary that we try to remind ourselves of as we talk about being present with gratitude and joy (they are also the words we use when describing our friendship): humility, inspiration, mindfulness, creativity, affirmation, kindness, laughter, hope, trust, respect, grit, determination, receptivity, serenity, honesty, and resilience. (I am only stopping because I ran out of breath.)

SANDY: And let's not forget optimism. You know that optimists really do live longer than pessimists.

WENDY: And probably happier, too. Okay here goes a story. I was travelling on a cruise with my husband. As is our pattern, we timidly and in collusion avoided the excursions of zip lines and cave explorations. Because we were tired and it was too hot, we decided not to walk back to the ship and so we bravely took the chairlift, which took us high into the air, the longest 10 minutes of our lives. We were awash in anxiety and fear. We made a conscious choice to combat our fear and to pursue the experience as one of pleasure. We discussed how our lives had been so good together; and-- right before we landed, and only because we had finally converted our perceptions from fear to joy-began to notice the beauty of the flora and fauna.

That night at dinner, a woman noticed my bracelet affirming my ride on the chairlift. I was talking about how risk taking we had been, how we made a point to change from fear to joy. She interrupted me to say that she had proactively *chosen* to go on the zip line and how during the entire ride, she and her husband were thrilled and kept saying they wanted to soak up every possible joy in life.

Sigh.

I mentioned to her that the ship's staff had asked people to sign up in advance for a special Chanukah celebration on the cruise. I suggested that it was probably for security. She insisted it was only to decide how much Manischewitz wine they had to order. Uh oh, I see a pattern here. Clearly I need to sit next to her more often.

SANDY: So, I wonder... do you want to choose the potential for joy even though it is sometimes scary? Can overcoming your fear feel like a joy in itself? When you told me this story, Wendy (and while I know you can reach for emotions of joy), I realized for the first time how much fear rather than pleasure or excitement you have about physically challenging yourself. I love that we are still learning new facts about each other after so many years of our friendship. When I go on my next adventure with Marc, I will make sure to regale you with every detail of our pleasure in the physical, as well as its safety, because I don't want you to be afraid or avoid the thrills that are possible when you travel.

WENDY: Helicopter rides, whale watching, hiking. Thanks so much. You are such a good influence, I am now thinking of going out without my shoes on. Truly, what is sweeter than being influenced by a friend in such a joyful way? No kidding, it makes a difference to me knowing your adventurous spirit could influence me.

But I swear, if you really try to influence me to do these things, the ukulele will be in the mail.

SANDY: How long does it take to recuperate from a concussion? (Mild, of course.)

WENDY: And you said you weren't funny? We have helped one another to continue to *Choose Joy*, haven't we! We have joy in our purpose, we have joy in our passions. And we have joy in our friendship.

Personally I know I will always complete my work, meet my deadlines, but I may not leave time for reading fiction (unless I have a book club) or listening to music without doing something else that is "productive." For those of you who resist joy, do your own analysis and make sure you program this into your life. It is so much easier when it is in place, by making it a habit rather than having to choose it - with all your resistance stopping you.

SANDY: And I know that I too may put so much time and energy into being my form of "productive" that I won't take time to notice the beautiful sunset that is glowing right outside my window. It helps so much when Marc reminds me. It helps so much when you remind me. Joy in beauty can be right there waiting and, unless I am mindful, I can miss it.

SANDY and WENDY: Here we are in harmony.

A good friend can help you feel joy about what already exists and coach you gently out of any slump. She will remind you to expand your universe.

We hope that in writing this book and sharing it with you, we will help you develop friendships that will drench you in joy as well.

Our suggestion: Take time to examine what, if anything in your life, may turn you away from feeling comfortable about pursuing pleasures- be they physical, sensual, intellectual or emotional. Our conversations as friends illuminate who we are, what we want or fear. They challenge us to pursue pleasure. Our friends encourage us to take risks, to do things that may bring us great joy if we overcome our fear.

Takeaway

- You can choose to practice gratitude ... once again, it takes an attitude adjustment first as well as practice.
- Once you have the habit of noticing and expressing appreciation for what life brings, it's important to share your experience with those around you. You then spread the joy.
- **A** good friend can help you choose and appreciate life's joys, reminding you of their positive benefits and actually enjoying them with you.

Epilogue

OUR BOOK IS finished.

We are still friends, closer than ever.

Friendship *matters*. We believe it even more deeply.

We have tried to give you a glimpse of our friendship. It is not meant to be copied. Aww, go ahead, copy it. Seriously, be yourself- and create a strong bond with a *friend for life* in a relationship that suits you both.

As therapists, we have seen that successful therapy often results in patients adding new and more intimate friends in their lives. We have observed what powerful sources of enrichment and strength these friendships have been. Friendships have enhanced our patients' lives. They continue the work we have done together "in the office" by reinforcing insights and healthy behavior "at home."

Our own unique friendship is an example of how we two people have learned to improve the quality of our lives through conversation, laughter, awareness, acceptance, challenge, and love.

And constructive criticism.

We plan to *good mother e*ach other *until death do us part.*

And longer, if necessary.

Acknowledgments

Wendy

FIRST OF ALL, I love love love my friend Sandy. (I am so good at understatement and she is saying *enough already*). She is like a personal trainer for my psyche. She knows me and loves me anyway (old adage) and makes sure I love myself (amendment.) She reliably listens and loves me.

I must thank our editor, Shulamit Falik, who I want as a friend. She gets us and is so skilled. She titillates my healthy narcissism with her warmth and affection as well as her excellent advice.

Ariel Rutland, you are a wonderful person and graphic designer and thank you for doing the cover of our book. Jennifer Yanowitz, you are a charismatic person and thank you for your clever ideas on ways to promote the book.

How can I ever thank my family and friends? Both groups fall under the friendship category.

There's my deep and true love - Jim, my very best friend, my heart, my soul. I adore him for all his kindness and love and intelligence. He makes me safe and contained and we wake up every morning laughing together. And he is damn sexy. (Sorry kids.) He really thinks about me and wants the best for me. What a good mother he is. (I do wish he would laugh at my jokes more.) And, he adds to the greater than good mother I had, my Anne Satin Shusterman.

Happily, he gave me one of my greatest gifts, a whole new family of his kids and their wives. *The Boys* - I think they really appreciate that's how we think of them. They are such a strong part of my happiness and stability. I love them, enjoy them and learn from them, intellectually and spiritually: Dean and Jen - Bruce and Teri and now our granddaughter, Chelsi, and her husband Scott and now Scottie Jr. And of course, friendship from Sue (*May she rest in peace*) and Irving as well as my beloved niece and nephew, Sharyn and Kevin.

Moving along to the *bride's* side, (When else can I think of myself that way?) There are my sisters Marcia Lavipour and Mary Ellen Schwab - my original and current best friends -and their special families. Marcia and Mary Ellen have always been the definition of loyalty, constancy, intelligence and love. I have so appreciated how they share their husbands (in a limited way) and their fabulous children. Marcia and David serve up Rachel and Dan, Sara and Scott with their jewels Jonah and Zachary and Michael and Sandy and their delicious Gabe. Mary Ellen and Bob bring me

Dan, Dahlia and latest hit - Dylan and Jennifer and Keith and their talented basketball team Alex, Jordan, and Jake.

That's an awful lot of Amazon Prime gift cards. And an awful, thankfully, lot of friends whom I admire and cherish.

I must acknowledge - the dearest friends who reviewed the book. I started first with Shelley Kushner and Marilyn Charwat- I knew they were going to love me anyway. It happily continued with Ellen Goldsmith, Elinor Goldberg, Carole Weinstein, Dean Rapaport, Bruce Rapaport, Mary Ellen Schwab, and Marcia Lavipour.

I never gave the book to Suzanne Pallot (sparing jealousy was my rationale.) Suzanne has been the kind of friend we are talking about for 44 years, special also because she had my mother for a teacher in 8th grade.

Special love to friends Mary High, Suzanne Wolfson, and Gary Kleiman - know and love them for 40 years, to Civi Lieberman and Carol Miller -whom I only have loved for 20 years and Marilyn Charwat and Shelley Kushner, each a mere loving 15 years.

Lucky for all the friends: my colleagues from the Diabetes Research Institute (Jay, Ron, Barbara, *etc.*); my brilliant professor of poetry- Kathleen Ellis; our writing instructor Kathrin Seitz; Suzanne, David and their daughter Eva; women from the book clubs in Maine and Boca Raton and the synagogue; my friends from the "Forum"; and all my "newer" friends from Rockland, Maine.

Thanks to the very special Suzi and Larry, Marilyn and Arthur, Civi and Alan, Carol and Ed, Bob and Bonnie, Carolyn and Mike, Rebecca and Nate and all my friends I have met professionally and love- starting with Dr. Susan Trutt.

And of course, to all my patients, past and future, I think the friendship like aspect of therapy - where you are entrenched in *good mother* glow- pleasurable for both parties -should always be supplemented by friendships in life.

And back to Jim, I know he is going to be a good sport about being in all my stories. Well anyway, in my dreams, he is smiling.

Sandy

Now I understand why so many Acknowledgement sections begin with the phrase, "This book couldn't have been written without..." It is very true. Writing a book can be a long labor of love but always is a long labor involving others. I could not have written this book without the support and assistance of so many.

My children, Merrick and Rachel and my daughter-in-law Shampa all read the book in its early incarnation, re-read it in its almost-final form and gave valuable feedback.

My sister Susan and her daughters Ariel and Amy also championed my efforts early on and later suggested ways to clarify concepts. (More about Ariel later.)

My friends were always supportive and in many instances went above and beyond. Ellen Feldman helped me to accumulate data about friendship. Lisa Horelick critiqued aspects of the book as part of our shared writing process. Both women thoughtfully read the book when it was completed and gave me their insights. My friends Aline Brandt, Steve Hyman, Dana Mindlin, MaryLou Ostling, and Judy Wilansky also read the completed manuscript and gave me their always helpful suggestions, as did my niece Sara. I know I am not mentioning other friends by name but please know that I value all of you for your friendship and truly couldn't have written a book from the heart about friendship without my involvement over many years with all of you.

I want to acknowledge the talent and skill of our book cover designer, Ariel Rutland (also my niece!) I believe she was able to bring to life in a visual, aesthetic way the essence of our book. A special mention to Shulamit Falik, our extraordinary editor. Right from the get-go she understood and appreciated what we were trying to say and helped us translate our meandering words into a clearer, more concise and more interesting book.

And two others without whom this book would not exist. To Wendy, my dear friend, thank you. Thank you for giving me the opportunity to participate in an incredible friendship, one of devotion and unwavering love and support. We have tried in this book to bring our friendship to life on the page, but words could never adequately describe our life-affirming relationship.

And talk about life-affirming relationships, I can never thank my husband and life partner enough for his encouragement, support and unbelievably valuable input, from the beginning concept for the book through to ideas for publication and marketing. Marc has been with me through countless hours at the computer, reminding me to go forward, reminding me to take breaks. In the book, as in my shared life with Marc, he continues to look out for me. As we say in the book, you want someone in your life who has your back. And Marc always has had and continues to have mine, lovingly. For that I am very, very grateful.

About the Authors

WENDY SATIN RAPAPORT, Psy.D., LCSW, is a clinical psychologist. She specializes in psychology-related facets of the health-care field, working with providers and patients. Dr. Rapaport is also an adjunct professor at the Diabetes Research Institute, part of the University of Miami Miller School of Medicine, and at the University of Maine Graduate School of Social Work. An interest in behavioral medicine and humor motivates her research, teaching, and writing. This is her fourth book.

Sanda Neshin Bernstein, Psy.D., is a clinical psychologist. She has worked in both school districts and universities. Dr. Bernstein is trained in psychotherapy, psychoanalysis, and as a school psychologist. She has a private practice where she sees both adolescents and adults. She has taught in Adelphi University's Postgraduate Program in Psychodynamic School Psychology. This is her first book.

Made in the USA
Middletown, DE
29 September 2017